Straight Up

A FINANCIAL GUIDEBOOK

Simple Straight Forward Advice Your Parents Never Gave You:

…because they probably don't know it themselves.

Rick Friedman

To Donna:

For putting up with all of my crap…love you

Table of Contents

Forward

Why Bother Reading this Guidebook?

If you're in your sixties or older, forget about it. You might as well give this guide to your children or grandchildren because you'll be doing them a huge favor. Your kid may be so grateful that he or she lets you move in if you end up broke. Fifties or forties, this guide can definitely help. You're a little late to the party, but you can still benefit. Thirties or twenties are excellent targets for the lessons contained here. You can easily secure a prosperous future. But Sweet Sally, if you're a teen and warmly embrace what I have to say, I absolutely promise you'll have a worry-free financial future.

I used to work in the financial industry selling a variety of financial products. When I first got into the industry, I did so with a strong academic background. More importantly, my parents had instilled a great deal of financial common sense. I was shocked to find out that very few of my clients were taught any of the lessons my parents shared with me. Worse yet, most didn't possess even the most basic understanding of day to day financial matters.

I would love to tell you that I've seen it all, but every month something new and more ridiculous came along. Two days before starting to write this guidebook (I started this little book while I still worked in the business), a client in his mid-forties cashed out of a retirement plan early. For those of you who do not know, this was a very costly decision. Ultimately, he paid penalties and taxes of more than 40 cents out of every dollar because of his age (too young). When I pressed him to find out why he needed to spend irreplaceable retirement money, he was reluctant to say. Eventually he confessed that he wanted to use the money to lease a car. Honestly, I was so shocked that I looked him in the eye and said "You've got to be fr@%king kidding me!" It's a good thing I'm 6'6" 240lbs because he wasn't especially happy to get my candid commentary. It was that moment I decided to write this guide. The title **Straight Up** is not a bartending reference; it's how I dispense my advice. All of my close friends know not to ask my opinion unless they're ready to hear exactly how I feel about a subject.

I may be coming off a bit rough and a tad callous. Here's the deal, I am about as honest as they come. Being painfully honest and selling financial products is not an ideal combination, but I scratched out a living while treating everyone fairly. Co-workers and clients alike knew they were going to get good advice whenever they asked me a question. So why did I write this guidebook? It boils down to three the things 1) I want you to succeed financially. 2) The part of the industry I enjoyed the most was educating people on personal finance, and 3) I'm lazy. It's a heck of a lot easier for me to give you the basics through this book, rather than talking with each of you individually.

I also have some great news. On top of being lazy, I'm mildly dyslexic which has made me pretty much hate reading. It takes me forever to get through anything longer than a fortune cookie, which means I could never write anything like one of the mountain of textbooks I've had to read in my life. This book is mercifully short and to the point. On top of that, if you haven't flipped through it yet, I even snuck in some pictures and other stuff to pad the size and make my guide appear longer than it really is.

If you're dead set against learning about your personal finances, but this was a gift from a relative who might sneak in a pop quiz, you can even cut this task down to about 10 minutes or less. Just look for definitions and key points in **bold italicized typeface**. For all you reluctant or resentful readers, stop reading the forward, scan the guidebook for bold passages, and you are good to go...but before you start skimming through the guide, let me tell you that reading this little guidebook cover to cover may make you rich.

To help you become wealthy you need to have a basic foundation of knowledge regarding your personal finance. I am not pitching any get rich quick schemes. This is not a manual on how to day trade stocks and options "risk free." No real estate deals where you can purchase homes for pennies on the dollar. No sure fire way to get government grants that you never have to pay back. What this book teaches is the basic principles that will insure you continually build your wealth until you decide you have enough. I want you to get to the point where you choose when you want to stop working. Some people never stop, but if you apply the principles outlined in this guide, then it'll be your choice. You will never be a slave to your financial condition.

I cannot tell you how much money is enough for you. Everybody has their own number. In all likelihood, a movie star or a professional athlete's number is different than yours or mine. It's up to you to decide how much is enough. My job here is to help you get to your number, whatever it happens to be. After you learn the process of growing your wealth, I am going to nag you about the most common pitfalls that trip up millions of people. These missteps can easily sabotage your financial future. They will be identified so they can be avoided.

The pages that follow are a compilation of lessons taught to me by my parents, through my MBA course work plus ongoing studies, from client interactions, and the stupid mistakes I made myself. As an advisor I saw a lot of financial mayhem. Let me tell you it's not much fun to run a financial plan for someone and then have to tell them they have only a slim chance to achieve their goals. The principles I provide apply to everyone regardless of how much money they currently or will eventually make. Don't fool yourself into thinking that if you work hard, are smart or talented enough, and have the drive to succeed in a high paying field that you are guaranteed a smooth ride into great wealth or a worry-free financial future. The sports and entertainment fields are littered with people who have made multiple millions of dollars only to lose it all.

Allow me to illustrate a good and bad example with some real clients from my practice. The names have been changed for obvious reasons. I worked with two gentlemen in their early sixties. The first one, John Smith, runs a gardening service. Most years he brings in about $60,000 from his business. He and his wife own their home and 4 rental properties worth over $1 million. He has close to $250,000 in savings and investments and all but one of his rental properties will be paid off by the time he plans to retire at age 66. John is set to live the life he wants. The other, Paul Jones is an accountant to professional athletes and B-list celebrities (yes, I do live in the Los Angeles area). Paul typically makes about $220,000 per year. He owns a home worth $800,000, but owes more than a half a million to the bank, and his total savings when we first met were $8,000. A man making that much money had only managed to save eight grand. Paul and his wife are screwed. They have some incredibly tough choices to make. Work indefinitely, health permitting, or drastically reduce the lifestyle they are used to living, perhaps they'll have to do both. Paul's biggest mistake was that he let time get away from him. Time is the key to building personal wealth. If you're young, time is your single best friend on the journey to financial success…let me show you how this works.

Chapter 1

Time is Money: The Rule of 72

Most of you have heard the expression "Time is Money." Nothing could be more true. This old adage can either be your best friend or your worst nightmare when we apply this to your personal finances. Let's start with the positive and talk about how your money can make more money. In business, we call it your return on investment, and in banking we call it interest. Simply put, *Interest is an amount of money someone will pay you for the use of your money.*

Let me give you an example. A co-worker walks up and starts telling you that his favorite band is coming to town and the tickets are selling fast. The tickets cost $89 and he's broke. He really wants to see the show, so he offers to pay you $100 on payday if you will lend him enough to buy his ticket today. You agree. Payday comes around and he gives you the $100 he promised. You promptly stash away the cash. The $11 extra dollars he gave you on payday was interest. Clearly, interest is a good thing here for you. You just scored an extra $11 just for letting someone use your cash. Now, for the other guy, the story isn't so good. But let's not talk about him now; we'll get back to being the payer of interest later in the guide.

So we know lending money to someone who will pay us interest is a good thing. If we stop and do some quick math here, we find that $11 extra bucks divided by the $89 you lent out is 0.124 or roughly 12% interest you earned on your money.

$$\frac{11}{89} = 0.124 \text{ rounded to } 12\%$$

Let just say our co-worker wants to see another show next month, but he's broke again. This time the tickets are $100 each. You were pretty pleased with the 12% you made last time, so you agree to lend him the $100 you stashed away if he'll pay you $112 on payday. Just like the last time, he comes through on his promise and pays you. Whether you realized it or not, two excellent things just happened here. 1) You made interest on your original $89 and 2) you also made interest on the $11 he paid you last time…Eureka… compound interest. *Compound Interest is when you earn interest on interest already paid to you.* If we break down our example, you made a total of $12 interest this time. $11 on your original $89 plus another $1 on the $11 of interest he paid the first time he borrowed money.

Here's where we add the very cool Rule of 72. This rule tells us how long it will take to double our money. *The Rule of 72: If you divide 72 by the compound interest rate, the answer you get is the number of times (or the length of time) you have to lend your money in order to double it.*

In our example, here's how the rule works:

$$\frac{72}{12\ (\%)} = \text{6 times or months to double your money}$$

At 12% interest per month, we double our money every 6 months.[i] Let's imagine that every month your coworker needs to borrow money for another concert and each concert ticket is 12% more expensive than the last one. If we start with your original $89, then you will see in the table below how your money will grow.

1 Concert 1 month	6 Concerts ½ year	12 Concerts 1 year	24 Concerts 2 years	48 concerts 4 years
$100	$178	$356	$1,424	$22,784

So after 4 short years of lending money to your co-worker, you've managed to grow your $89 bucks into an incredible $22,784. Make sure to note how much faster the money grew in the second two years of compounding compared to the first two. Time is money, boys and girls, never forget it.

Now we both know that the example we just went through is improbable at best. Don't get lost in the details, there are lessons to be learned. The key takeaways from this story are 1) *we want compound interest working for us* and 2) *the longer we allow our money to compound, the more beneficial it becomes*. Let's now take a more realistic approach to these concepts and see how we would apply them in our lives.

Chapter 2

Pay Yourself First

While it would be wonderful to make 12% interest a month and double your money every 6 months, it just isn't going to happen without risking a fairly lengthy prison sentence. Do an internet search on the name Bernie Madoff if you're too young to know who he is, and you'll know what I'm talking about. But there are many ways to get a reasonable rate of return if you're willing to take some risk. If I went into detail about all the ways to make your money grow here, then we would get terribly sidetracked. So for the purpose of illustration, I am going to ask you to take my word that about 7% growth per year over a long period of time is reasonable and achievable.[ii]

Recalling the Rule of 72, we would estimate that our money is going to more or less double every 10 years. If we start with that $100 we stashed away and calculate from your 20th birthday, you'd grow your cash to $200 at 30, $400 at 40, $800 at 50 and end up $1,600 at age 60. Heck that's not too bad, but hardly enough to pop the champagne and head to our yacht. Instead, let's see what happens if we commit ourselves to putting $100 from our weekly paycheck into our savings and investments paying us 7% a year. "Wait a minute," you're about to tell me. "I'm in high school or college, or just out of college and paying student loans, there is no way on earth I'm going to be able to squirrel away $100/week." Agreed, that's fair enough. Should we start with $50 or $25…still too much? Can you handle $5/week? If you tell me that's too much, then go to the nearest mirror, look closely and slowly say to yourself "I'm full of crap." If you baby-sit, mow lawns or recycle cans and bottles, you'll be able to save $5 bucks a week. Check out how all those amounts will grow over time at 7% annual interest.

	10 years	20 years	30 years	40 years
$5 / week	$3,762	$11,333	$26,570	$57,238
$25 / week	$18,804	$56,663	$132,851	$286,190
$50 / week	$37.61	$113,326	$265,702	$572,380
$100 / week	$76,079	$226,652	$531,405	$1,144,760

Each one of those boxes in the table represents a commitment we can make to ourselves and our future. Honestly, I really don't care which one you pick, all I insist is that you pick one now. We are in this together, so I just gave it some thought and chose my box, $50 per week for 20 years. Highlight it, circle it, or write the number on a piece of paper or on your bathroom mirror. Just pick one of those numbers and own it. That was the easy part, now we have to make it happen. We do that by paying ourselves first. *Paying yourself first means that you will treat adding to your saving as the single most important financial commitment in your life.* Before we pay the rent, student loans, car payment, cell phone bill, or shop for a new outfit, we will add to our savings. Unfortunately, it is incredibly easy to get off course and break our commitment. Things that we want or items we believe we need will always provide temptation.

Here's how I stay on track with my commitments, and I recommend you do the same. *Set up systematic (automatic) money transfers into savings and investments.* Retirement savings, college savings, vacation savings, general investments are all deducted directly from either my wife's or my paycheck or from one of our checking accounts. For me, I am so serious about satisfying my obligations to myself and my family's future that I time all my automatic investments to be sent out the same day my paycheck gets deposited. In that way, whenever I check my bank balances, I only see what remains after I've finished paying myself first.

I have one last point to make on this topic. It is extremely likely that over the course of time your pay will go up. Even though we picked a box today, *you can always choose to give yourself a raise.* While calculating various scenarios to present in this chapter, I took one from a financial plan of a married couple I worked with. They started 27 years ago with $25 a month in a single investment, then they added a second one. They went up to $50 on their way to $100 into each a few years later. Ten years later they added two additional investments and committed $200/each to all four. Currently, they add $1250 per month into their accounts on top of their retirement savings they each have at work. All in, they have over $1.7 million saved and when they hit their projected retirement date, they should have darn close to $3 million. Not bad for starting with $25 a month which is pretty close to that $5 a week we started with above.

So far we've talked about some very simple, but often ignored concepts. We need to pay ourselves first through automatic transfers. With that money we're paying ourselves, we will let it grow with investments that will give us compounding rates of interest or rates of return. The next thing we have to discuss is how to protect that money. Can you guess what represents the single biggest risk to your financial future? Go back to the mirror and have a look.

Chapter 3

The Bad Debt Trap: Live Within Your Means

Recall the guy you were lending money to so he could go see his concert? He represents the dark side of compound interest. What started out for him as a couple bucks extra to go see his favorite band spiraled into thousands of dollars. Sometimes we have to borrow money. Certainly, most of us can't pay cash for our first house. There are times when borrowing is necessary and good, but more often than not, **spending money we don't have can lead you to financial disaster.**

We're going to get started talking about debt, and I'm going to use myself as an example of what not to do. When I was fresh out of college, I screwed up big time. It started when I was walking across campus coming back from one of my last finals. I saw a table filled with cheap foam insulated beer, whoops, I meant soda can holders; you know the squishy ones that cost about a nickel to make. Also sitting on the table were stacks of credit card applications. A free can holder to fill out a 3 minute application, sweet deal, so I walked away with my cup holder and a week later my first credit card arrived in the mail.

The first month I paid my credit card bill in full. From there it went downhill. I continued to make a payment on-time every month, but I couldn't pay the bill in full. My credit card balance started to grow, and the card company loved me. They raised my credit limit and offered me more cards so I could dig myself in deeper, which I promptly did. The stupidity continued as I added store cards (department stores, electronics stores, gas stations, etc) to the mix. They all use the same tricks. If you open a store card, they'll give you a one-time discount. A gas card gave me cents off per gallon. The problem is that *if you don't pay off a credit card in full each time you get the bill, then you are going to pay much more for every item you buy with that card*. Remember how powerful the compound interest works to our advantage when we're saving? It's even more powerful when it works against you for the simple reason that the interest rates you pay for credit cards are far higher than the interest we are paid to invest. I see cards with rates at more than 24%. If you are ever late on a payment then you get nailed with the "penalty interest rate" which I have seen as high as 30%. Using the Rule of 72, every purchase left unpaid on a card with these rates will double in two to three years.

I reached my own breaking point in 1990. I accumulated $16,000 in debt. That may not sound like much to some of you, but keep in mind that this was at a time when movies tickets were about $4 bucks and gas was $1.25 a gallon. Since both movie tickets and gas are at least 3 times more expensive as of the writing of this book, I was really close to $50,000 in debt in 2014 dollars. I owed about 5 months wages, and still had rent to pay along with utilities, food, and gas. Carrying that much debt was extremely depressing. If you are there now, trust me, I feel your pain. If you haven't fallen into the trap, don't.

The best way to avoid this is to live within your means. *"To live within your means" can be translated to only spend money you have.* Credit cards make purchasing items very convenient, and it's a heck of a lot safer than carrying a bundle of cash wherever you go. If you are going to use credit, then you need to keep track of how much money you're spending, how much you have in your bank account, and how much your paycheck is going to be once deposited. I was frequently dumfounded by the number of people who had absolutely no clue how much money was either coming in or going out of their bank accounts at any given time. Understand what bills are going to be coming over the course of the month and don't spend too much of your available cash on big ticket items (TV, trips, furniture) or lifestyle items (food, entertainment, clothing, toys). You will also find that if you save up for those big ticket items rather than purchasing them on credit, you'll end up buying fewer of them, and those that you do buy will bring you more pleasure.

For those of us who have already made the mistake of going into debt, take heart, there are some ways out. For left brain analytical thinkers, here's the most rational way to get out of debt. Take all of your credit cards out of your wallet except for the one with the lowest rate which will go back into the wallet FOR EMERGENCIES ONLY. From now on you will ONLY PAY CASH for your purchases. This is quite inconvenient, but necessary to retrain yourself how to spend more wisely. Now make a list of all your credit card debt and order it by interest rates, highest to lowest. Pay the minimum payment on every card except the one on the top of your list which has the highest interest rate. Pay as much as you can on that high rate card until it's paid off completely. Once it's paid off, take every penny that you were paying to the first plus the minimum payment you were already making on card number two. Do that until card number two is paid off and then apply everything to number three and so on down the line. This method will minimize the total amount of interest you pay.

I took a more right brained approach to get myself out of debt. I followed the same steps I outlined above, but instead of ordering the debt from highest to lowest interest rate, I ordered mine by balance or amount owed. I paid off my smallest balance first until eventually I got down to my largest balance. While this method did not minimize the total interest I paid, it provided emotional reinforcement. My smallest balance was a department store card with about a $250 balance. So, after two months I was already onto card number two. It was a quick victory that powered me to take on the next and then the next. After seven more cards, I was finally out of credit card debt forever. I promise you that I still remember the unbridled joy I had when I made that last payment. I have never run a balance on a credit card since, and will never do it again. Coincidently, that last credit card I paid off was that first college credit card. I guess that ended up to be one of the most expensive insulated can coolers in the history of modern man.

At the beginning of this chapter, I mentioned that there are some necessary or good types of debt, let's take a look at those now.

Chapter 4

Good Debt: Sound Investments in Your Financial Future

There are only two things worth going into debt for: higher education and real estate. The reasons why these two items are worth going into debt are twofold. First, both can put you on a stronger financial path, and second the interest you pay to the bank on student loans and loans to purchase a home (mortgage) are currently deductible from your income taxes. I know we haven't talked about income taxes yet, but there will be a full explanation in a Chapter 6.

Let's start with the life choice of whether or not to go to college. If you're already in the working world, is it worth the time, money and effort to get a degree? Since I am a numbers guy, let's look at the basic statistics. According to the US Department of Education, *male adults ages 25 to 34 with a bachelor's degree earn 55% more than those without, and similarly, women earn 60% higher salaries.*[iii] Obviously, there are plenty of exceptions to the rule, but when you're planning for your future, play the odds and get the degree. There are so many companies that require a college diploma to consider you for a job or promotion, that you would be foolish to limit yourself by choice.

There are hundreds, if not thousands of majors to choose from, which should you choose and when should you go to college? At this point I could start rolling off a list of fields of study that typically generate the highest incomes, but I won't. Most of your parents would also recommend that you go off to college immediately after high school (mine did), and I'm not going to do that either. The reason being is that a college degree requires a huge commitment of time, effort and money, so my advice is going to be a little different than what the "experts" or your parents might recommend.

If you're an athlete who's been offered a scholarship, then take the money and run, shoot, bat or whatever talent got you the money and get your degree now. If you're an exceptional academic performer **and you are certain** that you want to become a doctor, engineer or the like, then go go go. If you are not certain of your career path, then my recommendation would be to wait. I have many friends and acquaintances that earned bachelor's or advance degrees in a field only to find out that they hate the business they chose. They ended up pissing all that time and money away…bad call. If you only think you want to work in a field, get an entry level position and find out whether your chosen field is right for you. If it is, great, you can throw your efforts into college and maybe your employer will cover some or all of the expense. If it's not a field you want to pursue, then you just saved yourself from a ton of debt and wasted time.

In my case, I went to college when I was still 17 years old. I got accepted into one of the most prestigious universities on the west coast because my coach was friends with the coach at the university. I mailed my application to the gymnasium and bingo, I was in. Unfortunately, I lacked the focus and discipline to really take advantage of the opportunity presented me and squandered it away. I did get my degree, but it was in a field that was virtually useless and my GPA was mediocre at best. Had I the opportunity to roll back the clock, I would have joined the military first, learned discipline and perhaps would have found direction for my career path much sooner. Once I did find a new path, I went back to school to earn an MBA. I was a recognized top performer in my class, my company had a modest tuition reimbursement program, and many new doors were opened.

If either your parents or you are insistent on heading to college immediately after high school, but you're not the brainiest or a star athlete, then consider a college or university with a work study program. By doing so, you'll be able to test drive the jobs in your chosen field of study while pursuing your degree. The bottom line is that higher education can really help your financial future, but do yourself a favor. Before you go, make sure that you know why you are doing it. Ideally, have a passion for the field you are pursuing. If you do, then the enormous investment of time, effort and money is more likely to reap you great rewards.

*****

Real estate is the other investment worth taking on the burden of debt. Very few of us are going to be able to pay cash for a house, so we are going to need to borrow most of the money. As mentioned above, the interest you pay on your mortgage is currently a tax deductible expense and therefore, we have categorized it a good debt. There are many types of mortgages out there, but at this point I want to focus entirely on the most common which is a 30 year fixed rate loan. On this type of loan, you pay 360 monthly mortgage payments (30 years x 12 month per year = 360 payments). The loan payment amount will never change over the term of the loan, hence the "fixed rate" terminology. Even though the payment never changes, the ratio of interest (cost to borrow) and principal (amount borrowed) does. Using the mortgage on my current home, here's how it breaks down:

Loan Amount	$378,000
Interest Rate	4.125%
Term (months)	360
Payment	$1,831.98

Now look at the break down of principal and interest for our payment:

	Amount Owed	Interest Portion	Principal Portion	New Balance
First Payment	$378,000.00	$1,299.38	$532.60	$377,467.40
After 5 years	$342,577.07	$1,177.61	$654.37	$341,922.70
After 10 years	$299,055.54	$1,028.00	$803.97	$298,251.56
After 15 years	$245,583.86	$844.19	$987.78	$244,596.08
After 20 years	$179,887.18	$618.36	$1,213.61	$178,673.57
After 25 years	$99,170.54	$340.90	$1,491.08	$97,679.47
After 30 years	$0.00	$0.00	$0.00	$0.00

There is only one thing you need to note from the table above. ***When paying on a mortgage, the large majority of your payment goes towards interest in the early part of your loan.*** In fact, after 5 years of payments totaling close to $110,000, we will only pay off about $35,000 with the other $75,000 being interest to the bank. Over time, the ratio switches. Look at the last 5 years. Out of the same $110,000 in payments $99,000 will go to paying back what we borrowed and only $11,000 in interest. Over the course of paying off our mortgage, we will pay a total of $659,511.36 of which a staggering $281,511.36 will be interest. We do get the tax advantage of paying all that interest, but wouldn't it be better to not pay so much interest?

Here is what I recommend you do when you're paying off your mortgage. Pay more than the required payment. Any extra payment you make will go directly to paying off the amount you initially borrowed (principle portion). This is what we call building equity.

Equity is the amount something is worth less the amount you owe. On our first home, my wife and I added about $25 to each payment to speed the repayment of the loan. On our current home, we rounded the $1831.98 payment up to $2000 even. Look at the table below and see what happens because we add extra to our mortgage payment.

	Amount Owed	Interest Portion	Principal Portion	New Balance
First Payment	$378,000.00	$1,299.38	$532.60	$377,467.40
After 5 years	$331,401.90	$1,139.19	$860.81	$330,541.10
After 10 years	$274,150.28	$942.39	$1,057.61	$273,092.67
After 15 years	$203,809.45	$700.59	$1,299.41	$202,510.05
After 20 years	$117,386.90	$403.52	$1,596.48	$115,790.42
After 25 years	$11,205.92	$38.52	$1,961.48	$9,244.44
Paid in full in 25.5 years				

In this table, I want you to take notice of a couple items. Comparing the "Amount Owed" on this table to the prior one, you can see how much faster we are paying off the loan and building equity. In the first 5 years we have paid down an extra $11,000. After 15 years of the increased payments we have accumulate about $42,000 ($244,596.08 - $202,510.05 = $42,086.03) more equity. The other item to note is that we have completely paid off the loan 4.5 years early. By not having to pay the last 54+ payments totaling $99,591.26, we have effectively saved ourselves close to $50,000 in interest that we would have had to pay to the bank.

Now that I have overloaded you with numbers and tables, I want to bring this all back to the context of building your financial future. Buying real estate is one of the single best ways to build your financial future. I ran hundreds of financial plans, and virtually all of my *clients with more than one piece of real estate were more financially secure than those without real estate holdings*. There is a simple reason for that. Real estate can increase your wealth and your spendable cash. I know what you're thinking, making one mortgage payment looks like a huge commitment, how in heaven's name am I going to be able to pay on two or more?

Let's take the example of a friend who owns two houses. When he moved into his second home he decided to hold onto his first house. Instead of selling, he rents it out to a group of friends. There are four of them who pay a total of $2000/month. His mortgage is $1200 and other expenses run about $600 per month. So, he makes $200 spendable cash every month, but more importantly *his renters are buying the house for him*. Once the mortgage is paid off, he or you can use the cash as an extra or retirement income. Another option is to borrow against the equity in your current real estate to buy another property. You could continue to do that indefinitely. Imagine if you had five or ten properties that generate the same rent and have the same expenses as our example. You would be making $2000 a month in extra income now, and once paid off, then you would be making $20,000 a month and be a real estate mogul and millionaire.

Clearly, I have made the case for why taking on debt for real estate can be a huge advantage in creating a financially secure you, but it's not all glitz and glamour. Like every investment, there are positives and negatives, and when it comes to the negatives, real estate certainly has its share and more (I will list some of those pitfalls in Chapter 13). The one investment that has virtually no downside is investing in your own education. No matter what happens to you in life, nobody can take away your knowledge and experience. So make these two investments in education and real estate even though they will require you to take on what could be massive debt. Trust me…they'll pay off.

Now we understand the basics of good debt (tax deductible and good investments for our financial security) and bad debt (not tax deductible for expenditures on lifestyle items). Interest rates can vary widely even when we are asking to borrow for the same item. Why, for instance, is my mortgage interest 4.125% when others are paying over 6.5% for the same type of loan? One of the biggest determiners of whether someone will loan to us and how much interest they will charge is our *credit score*. Of all the factors, this is the one we can most control.

Chapter 5

Your Credit Score: The Ins and Outs of Building a Great Score

When we buy anything on credit, the interest charged is the extra cost we pay for the use of someone else's money (remember our concert goer). The actual interest rate we pay is based on a number of factors. One of those factors is whether the loan is secured or unsecured. When a loan is backed by something the lender can take back from the borrower and resell (house or car), this is called a secured loan. When we buy clothes or food on credit this is called an unsecured loan because the lender can't easily take back and resell a meal or an outfit (did you get any visuals on that?). The rates on secured loans tend to be lower than for unsecured loans. Rates within the secured and unsecured universes can still vary greatly. Using credit cards as an example, I've seen rates as low as 8% and as high as 24%. What determines the rates we are offered? One big factor is our credit score. There are a handful of rating agencies that keep track of our credit and payment histories and give each of us a score that is meant to predict the likelihood that we will pay back what we borrow. The higher the score, the more likely we are going to pay our loans back (i.e. less risk to the lender) and therefore the lower the interest rate we have to pay to borrow.

The credit rating agencies use 5 factors to calculate our scores. I am going to list them here by level of importance, with the most important coming first. Not surprisingly, our payment history on past debt is the biggest single factor and represents 35% of our total score. Did we pay back past debt; have we always been on time making our payment? These are terribly important. ***Never miss a payment even if it's just the minimum amount due, and never make a payment late.*** As I mentioned in the chapter on bad debt, if you are late on a credit card payment, the rates skyrocket, and you'll also have to pay a late charge on top of it. The credit card companies are making a ton of money already; don't give them the opportunity to make even more. If this book has found you later in life and you are struggling to make ends meet, then consider the following if you have to choose what bills are going to get paid on time. When calculating your score, late or missed payments on a home or student loan are more damaging to your credit than is a late credit card bill. Even though the penalties and interest are higher for missing credit card payment, if you are trying to maintain the best possible credit which you should, then late pay the credit card bill.

The second biggest factor in determining your credit score is your total amount of debt outstanding. This accounts for 30% of your credit score. Credit rating agencies negatively view credit card debt compared to other types (mortgage, student or vehicle). So again, the more credit card debt you carry, the lower your credit score is going to be. You also want to manage the total amount of credit that you have available to you. I recall my wife and I applied for a mortgage and were turned down initially. Even though our credit scores were in the excellent range, my access to credit was too high. Remember that can holder credit card I have? Over the course of 20 years, the card company had been increasing my credit limit. At the time we applied for the mortgage, the limit on that card was north of $25,000. The mortgage lender didn't want to risk me maxing out the card after I took on their mortgage, hence the reason for the denial. The problem was easily fixed. I called the credit card company and asked them to lower the limit to $10,000; problem solved...we got the mortgage. Even though it's tempting and an ego stroke to amass a great deal of available credit, resist the urge because it can backfire.

Here's one final factor to know on this element of our credit score. Rating agencies view running a credit card balance greater than 30% of our available limit either in total or per individual card as a negative. For example, if I have 2 credit cards with $1,000 limit on each, then my credit score will go down if I own more than $300 on either card or $600 in total. This won't be a factor for you because you're going to heed all my advice, but it must be mentioned so you know how your credit score works. To summarize, for this very important element of your credit score; ***don't take on more debt than you can easily handle and don't fill your wallet with cards you don't need or use***.

The last three factors of your credit score are not nearly as important or controllable as the first two. Coming in at 15% of your total score is the length of your credit history. As someone new to this world, it is impossible to have a perfect score regardless of your income. So don't sweat it. Get yourself a credit card and treat it responsibly. The first will be the hardest one to get (unless you run into a table with foam insulators). Once you have established your first account and have proven yourself worthy, the offers for more cards and credit will come very quickly. Use caution my friend. Don't forget that if you have too much available credit you may get turned down for an important loan like what happened to me.

The last two factors are each worth 10% towards your total credit score. They are called new credit and credit mix. For the new credit element, ***applying for too many cards too*** *quickly is considered a red flag* for credit issuers. Is the person opening all these new lines because they are in financial trouble? Since the banks don't know why you need more new lines of credit, your score can fall if you apply for a lot of new credit in a short period of time. Credit mix is an odd category which is derived from what types of credit you have been able to successfully manage. Credit issuers like to see that an individual can manage different types of debt. Was the borrower able to handle her student loan, car payment and credit card without missing or being late? Again, you don't have a heck of a lot of control over this element, and it is a relatively minor component. Keep yourself focused on the first and biggest two elements of your credit score. Once you get the ball rolling and you manage the two biggies well, you will be able to borrow whenever you need.

Well we've covered a lot of ground and we still haven't gotten to the fun stuff of investing and making money. Don't worry we're getting close. Before we are able to invest, we need to earn an income. If you're earning an income you better know a little bit about income taxes.

Chapter 6

Income Taxes: Why Is My Paycheck So Much Less Than What I Earned?

I've got to start with a warning that this is a very dry and boring chapter. You're probably thinking, "Oh God, how could this book get any worse?" Unfortunately, we have to do this because the stuff contained in this chapter will cement some of the items in the last chapters and provide a framework for the information that is yet to come. So I'll ask for your patience and advise you to swig down some coffee or an energy drink. With that disclaimer, let's get started.

For those of us already in the working world we see the impact of taxes on our paychecks every month. For those of you who have not landed that first job, here's a warning. If you get a job that pays $12/hour for 40 hours per week, congratulations, you will be earning 480 bucks a week; that's your gross pay. ***Be warned, when you get the check it's going to be a lot less***. I found one of my wife's old paycheck stubs (sorry honey) that showed that she grossed $3,015.99 and her take home pay was $2,183.63. That's a whopping $832.36 taken out of her check. The main reason for the difference was taxes. From every paycheck the state and federal government gets their share first. They'll deduct

Federal Income tax, State Income tax (there are 41 states that have this), Local income tax (there are areas in 14 states and Washington DC that levy this tax), Social Security tax, Medicare tax, State Unemployment Insurance tax and finally State Disability Insurance tax. If I missed one from your state then you have my apologies. Man-o-man that's a lot of different taxes and helps explain why our take home pay is less than our gross pay.

The following is a list of each tax and its purpose. The first four on the list below are calculated by formula. There is no way to change the amount or timing of how those are taken from our paychecks.

State Disability Insurance tax: Deducted from your paycheck to pay benefits to people who were injured and cannot return to their the job.

State Unemployment Insurance tax: Deducted from your paycheck to pay a portion of income for those who were laid-off from their job. *FYI, if you voluntarily leave or are fired for cause (violated the terms of your employment), you are not entitled to unemployment benefits.*

Medicare tax: Deducted from your paycheck to pay a portion of the healthcare expenses for retired and/or disabled people.

Social Security tax: Deducted from your paycheck to pay retired people who have worked enough time to qualify. Social security pays retirees a lifetime income. The actual benefit amount depends on the number of years paying into the system and your income during that time.

State and Local Income tax: If you live in a state or municipality that has this, then this tax is collected to help fund the general operations of the state or municipality including, education, public safety, transportation, etc.

Federal Income tax: Just like the state tax, this money is collected to help run our country. Since this represents the largest portion taken from our paychecks and we have some control over it, we're going to spend extra time to understand this one a little more fully. Tax laws are extremely complex, so I am going to omit a lot of detail and nuance in order to give you a general understanding. Take a look at the graph below. It shows the income tax rate for a single person in 2012.

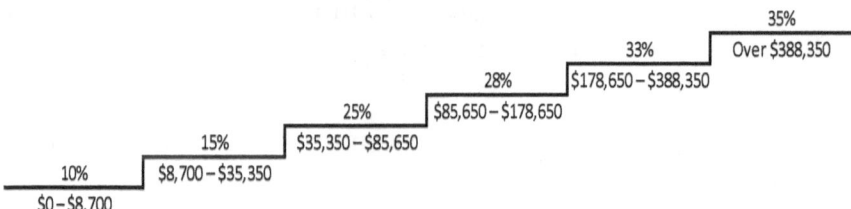

Income taxes are designed like a staircase. In 2012, every dollar of your income up to $8,700 was taxed at 10 percent. The very next dollar (and each one after until you hit the next stair at $35,350) was then taxed at 15%. It is important to understand that if your income for the year ends up on that second stair, you only owe 15% for the amount over $8700; that first block of income will always be taxed at the lowest rate, which was 10%. This holds true no matter how many steps you take on the staircase. Look at the table below that shows the federal income tax for Joe, single guy who made $30,000 in 2012.

Tax Rate	Taxable Income	Taxes Owed
10%	$8,700	$870
15%	$21,300	$3,195
TOTALS	$30,000	$4,065

Fortunately, when Joe filed his taxes, the news got better. From his gross income he got to deduct a chunk of money called either his **standard deduction** or **itemized deduction**. For 2012 the standard deduction was $5950. With the standard deduction Joe's taxes would have ended up as follows:

Tax Rate	Taxable Income	Taxes Owed
10%	$8,700	$870
15%	$21,300	$3,195
Deduction	-$5,950	-$893
TOTALS	$24,050	$3,172

He could have still done better. Remember the discussion on good debt (Chapter 4) when we talked about deducting the interest from student loans and mortgages? If your tax deductible expenses exceed your standard deduction, then you get to deduct the higher amount. Let's assume that Joe had a mortgage of $800/month of which $600 was interest. He paid real estate tax of $1000/year. On top of that he paid on his student loans a total of $300/month where $200 was interest. If we add these all together ($7200 mortgage interest + $1000 property tax + $2400 student loan interest), then we get $10,600 as his itemized deductions. Since his itemized deductions were higher than his standard deduction, Joe got the larger itemized amount. The table below shows Joe's taxes using the itemized deduction.

Tax Rate	Taxable Income	Taxes Owed
10%	$8,700	$870
15%	$21,300	$3,195
Deduction	-$10,600	-$1,590
TOTALS	$19,400	$2,475

So by making sound investments in his financial future, Joe got the added benefit of saving about $700 on his taxes ($3,171 tax using the standard deduction - $2,475 tax using the itemized deduction = $697 tax savings). Remember, I have vastly simplified this example, and intentionally ignored other items that may change your income taxes.

Once you file your taxes not later than April 15th of the following year, you will either pay what you under paid in federal tax during the year, or receive a refund check if you paid in more than you owe over the course of the year. The same is true for your state income tax.

The Internal Revenue Service (IRS: the federal tax agency) considers income taxes as a "pay as you go" system. Kind of like a cell phone bill or gym membership where we pay every month, taxes are deducted from every paycheck we receive. *How much tax is withheld depends on us*. When we do all the paperwork for a new job, one of the forms is called a W-4. It tells our employer how much income tax to withhold based on our **filing status** and the **number of exemptions** we claim. Your filing status is simple. You just declare whether you're married or single. If you are married and you both work, the lower income spouse should claim single to make sure enough taxes are withheld. The number of exemptions is basically claiming how many people the income is supporting. If you're single and living alone, you would claim "Single 1" on your W-4. If you're married and your spouse doesn't work, then you will claim "Married 2." If you also have a child, then claim "Married 3." There is no legal requirement to claim what is your actual life situation, but beware.

Joe is a smart guy and he's going to embrace all my advice. He is thinking I'm going to save more than enough to pay my taxes at the end of the year, so why not claim "Married 20"? By doing so, there will be very little income taxes withheld from his paycheck, and he would get the benefit of the use of his money plus all the interest or earnings that his money produces. The problem happens when he files his taxes. If Joe has shorted the IRS by more than 10% of what he owes (in Joe's case if he owes more than $248 on his return), then the IRS will levy a fine and make him pay estimated taxes every quarter the following year. *We always want to avoid fines, its wasted money*. So do your best to get your tax withholdings close to your tax bill. In a perfect world, you would owe about 9% of your total tax each year. However, I would not recommend playing it that close. If you're a good saver, shoot for a $0 tax return by matching your filing status and number of exemptions to your actual situation. If you are a lousy saver, then you may want to intentionally over withhold (claim fewer exemptions than you are entitled). If you employ this strategy, then once you file your return, you will receive a large dollar amount as a tax refund. You could then put this money towards savings. Try to avoid this; it's much better to save throughout the year and develop a savings discipline that will serve you a lifetime.

While we're on the topic of taxes and saving, there is a far too often ignored strategy that can help you do both. Many employers out there offer retirement plans called 401k's, 403b's or less common ones called SEP IRA's or Deferred Compensation plans. Thanks to my father, I've participated in these plans in every job I've held since completing my undergraduate degree. Let's spend a little time understanding how these can lower your taxes and build your savings.

Chapter 7

Employer Retirement Plans: Easiest Way to Build a Nest Egg

I just mentioned that I have my father to thank for getting me going on my retirement savings. Here's how it happened. I was in my early 20's and working for a hotel company in San Francisco. The company was rolling out a new program to all the employees called a 401K. I was absolutely not interested in participating because I did not want to limit my discretionary spending (i.e. cut into my beer budget). Fortunately, I told my dad about the program and also told him that I wasn't going to do it. Thank goodness he told me I would be a ding-dong if I chose not to take advantage of this company benefit. First question he asked me was, "Does the company plan to match your contribution?" I told him that they were going to match 50 cents on the dollar for the first two percent and 25 cents for the second two percent. Next he asked me if I knew that the money came out before taxes. I said, "yea...so what?" He then explained that I would not have to pay income taxes on the money I put in the plan, so my take home pay would not be much lower than I was used to getting. Ultimately, we made a deal. I would put 5% into the 401K, and if the impact was too big, then I would discontinue my participation. The results were amazing.

First and foremost, my take home pay was hardly impacted. My paycheck was only about $20 less than it had been and I was putting about $50 into the plan every week. My experience was not unique. A husband and wife were clients of mine. He was a retired law enforcement officer and she worked for a multinational corporation as an executive assistant to the president. She made great money, but never put money into her 401K despite an extremely generous company match. I went through the same conversation as I had with my father 20 years earlier and we made the same deal. A few weeks later she called absolutely ecstatic. She told me that her take home pay actually went up despite making the contribution. In her case, making the pre-tax contribution moved her to a lower step on the income tax staircase. Of those who I've convinced to start making contributions into their company retirement plan, not even one told me it was a bad move.

There are a couple of ideas you should take away from these stories. **Make the commitment to participate in a company retirement plan. By doing so, you will lower your tax bill and if your company matches you'll also get free money.** Free money is yours for the taking if your employer provides a company's match. Think about how it worked for me when I worked at the hotel. I contributed 5% of my gross pay. To simplify, let's call it $5. Recall the match the company was offering: 50 cents on the dollar for the first two percent and 25 cents for the second two percent. So for every $5 put in the plan, the company added $1.50. If we do the math on that, the company match was the equivalent to getting an investment return of 30%. Give yourself a raise on the company's dime by doing nothing more than to opt to participate in the plan. If your company has a matching retirement plan, then you would be a fool not to **contribute at least the minimum amount to capture the entire** *company match.* If your company matches two percent, then you contribute at least two percent. If the company matches seven percent, then you contribute at least seven percent.

What's the catch to get this free money? Like everything in life, you never get something for nothing. Your retirement plan is no different. There are two rules with which you need to be aware. One is company enforced and the other is from the IRS. Your company is going to impose what is called a vesting schedule. A vesting schedule is how long you must work for the employer before the company match becomes yours. There are two types. 1) **Cliff vesting**: all of the company match becomes yours after a specified number of years of service. My last employer cliff vested after 3 years of service. If I work for 2 years and 11 months, all the money the company put into my 401K goes back to my employer. Three years or more service, it all belongs to me. 2) **Graded vesting**: the company matching funds become yours incrementally over the course of several years. The hotel vested 25% of their match per year of service. After four years of service the entire match became vested. I worked there for over 6 years, so I was entitled to take all the company funds when I ended my employment. If I had only worked there two years, then I would have been able to take half of the match. Understand that *the dollars that you earn and opt to defer are not subject to vesting. If the cash came out of your pay, then it's always yours...period.* Don't use vesting as an excuse not to participate. I don't care if you say that you're only going to be there for a year or two. You never know where your life path is going to take you. If you end up giving back the entire company match, so be it. If you get some or all of the free money...congratulations!

The other catch to putting money into a retirement account is that surprisingly, the IRS expects people to use the money for retirement. While there are some exceptions including taking out money for the purchase of your first home, generally, if you take money out before you hit the age of 59 ½, then there is a steep penalty. Taking money out before that magic age will subject you to a 10% penalty + the amount is added to your income for the year. Recall that guy from the beginning of the book who cashed out $4,000 of his retirement plan to lease a car? He was in the 25% federal and 9.3% state income tax brackets, then add the 10% penalty for taking the money before 59½. That's 44.3% or $1772 of his $4000 was spent on taxes and penalties, which left him $2,228 to lease that stupid car. You can understand why I was so angry with him. It was very expensive money. Bottom line for these or any other types of retirement accounts is that the money is not for you. I have always had the outlook that every penny that goes into my retirement account is not for me, rather it's for Old Man Rick. Since there has always been outside savings, I have never been tempted to use the money.

To summarize the main points of this chapter, 1) participate in any company sponsored retirement plan. 2) All the contributions you make are deducted from your taxable income for the year. 3) If your company matches part or all of your contribution, then contribute at least enough to capture all of the free money available to you. 4) Have the mindset that this is not a regular saving account; all money saved is dedicated to your retirement, and never sooner than 59½. What if your company doesn't offer a retirement plan? If that's the case, then you are on your own to start saving for retirement. You can do this through an Individual Retirement Account called an IRA.

Chapter 8

Individual Retirement Accounts: Doing it Yourself

So what happens if your employer doesn't set up a retirement plan for its employees? It's up to you. The way an individual is able to save for his or her retirement is through a special account called an Individual Retirement Account or IRA. The biggest difference between an IRA and a 401K is that the contributions cannot be taken directly out of your paycheck. You'll have to report the contribution when you file your taxes. For a 401K, the contribution is deducted and reported by your employer on a year-end form called a W-2. The other difference between the two is the contribution limits to an IRA are not as generous as what you are able to put into a 401K plan. The 2012 contribution to your 401K was limited to $17,000 for folks under 50 and $22,500 if you were 50 years or older. For an IRA the limits were $5,000 under 50 and $6,000 for 50 and older. For our purposes here, those are the only important differences between the two.

There are many choices where you can set-up an IRA account. Most banks, credit unions and investment firms (including online providers) are going to be able to set up an IRA account for you. I am not going to go into the advantages and disadvantages of each choice at this point because we'll get to that topic once we've talked about investing.

When you do pick the institution to set up your IRA account, the first question the banker or representative is going to ask is, "What type of IRA do you want to set up today, Traditional or Roth?" This is a little confusing, so stay with me. *In a traditional IRA (or regular 401K), you are able to deduct the amount you contribute off your current year's income.* So, if you make $30,000 income for the year and you put the full $5,000 into your Traditional IRA, you'll only pay taxes as if you made $25,000. The catch comes when you are retired and you start drawing funds off your IRA account. When you do, every penny of what you put in and all of the growth in the account is taxable in the year you take it out. The basic theory of the Traditional IRA is that when you are retired, your income tax percentage will be lower than when you were working. If this is the case, then you'll pay less tax on your IRA savings in retirement than the year(s) you originally earned it.

The Roth IRA works exactly the opposite as the Traditional IRA. All of your contributions are still taxable in the year you earned the money. Using that last example, you make the same income and contribute $5,000, but this time you choose a Roth IRA. In this case, you'll pay taxes like you made $30,000 this year. Where's the benefit you ask? It comes when you are retired. *As long as you are 59½ when you start pulling money out of your Roth, every penny of your contribution and earnings on those contributions are completely tax free!!* Remember my financial commitment to myself in Chapter 2? If not, it was $50/week for twenty years. Let's do the math on this example and assume those weekly contributions were going into a Roth IRA. Over 20 years at $50/week, I would have put in a total of $52,000, but as the table showed, that money will grow to an estimated $113,326. If this is what actually happens, then I will be able to spend the entire $113,326 in retirement without paying anything in taxes on the $61,326 of growth in the account. That's the benefit of Roth IRA...tax-free earnings on our money. One note to be aware. Many company 401K plans offer a Roth option that works the same as I just described. Just know the difference when you are enrolling in a company sponsored plan. ***The Roth option is pay taxes now and get your money out tax free at retirement, and a regular 401K (or traditional IRA) you save on your taxes today and you pay when you retire.***

So which do you choose? That is a very complicated question which includes making guesses at what both your future income and the future tax rates are going to be over the next several decades. With that disclaimer in place, it really boils down to a best guess. If you think your earnings are going to be substantially less once you retire, then you'll end up taking one or more steps backwards on the income tax staircase. Save on taxes today when your tax rates are higher and pay later when your taxes are going to be lower. If this is your guess, choose a traditional IRA. If you are not likely to see a dramatic drop in income once you retire, then the Roth may be the better choice. I wish I had a crystal ball or an absolute rule of thumb to give you here, but it is a rather complicated issue that should be made on a case by case basis. Many folks choose to split their contribution half Roth and half traditional; I would not argue against that strategy. Regardless of your choice, just make the commitment to yourself and open an IRA if you do not have a retirement plan at work.

Finally, I am going to bring you back once again to Chapter 2. Make your contributions automatically from your bank or credit union to your IRA throughout the year. There are two advantages to automatic investments. 1) If you give yourself the opportunity, you may miss making a month's or a year's contribution. Don't give yourself the option to sabotage your own financial future. Every time a paycheck gets deposited, there should be an automatic contribution into your IRA, just like what would happen if you have a company sponsored plan. 2) By setting up automatic investments, you get to invest at multiple points throughout the year rather than just at one point if your IRA is funded all at once. This is called "dollar cost averaging" and it's an important part to sound investing. We will be discuss dollar cost averaging in more detail in Chapter 13.

Did I just use the word "investing?" Yes, I did. At long last we have finally made it to the fun stuff that gets airplay on the TV and makes computer headlines every day. It makes sense to talk about this now. We know that we want to make interest and/or earnings on our money instead of spending it all or stashing it in a shoebox. We have agreed to pay ourselves first, so we're building up our saving. We are going to avoid creating a debt burden on lifestyle purchases. We will buy real estate and invest in higher education. We've set up our retirement accounts either through work or on our own at a financial institution. So what are we going to do to get our money working for us? Let's find out.

Chapter 9

Investing Your Savings: Stocks, Bonds and Cash

Investing our money can be a pretty tricky proposition. There are so many choices. Savings accounts, certificates of deposit, stocks, bonds, mutual funds, closed-end funds, exchange traded funds, unit investment trusts, real estate investment trusts, limited partnerships, variable insurance policies, annuities; the list goes on and on. Most folks find the process of learning about all the choices overwhelming. As a result, they get paralyzed and end up doing nothing with their money and miss out on profits that are available to them. It has taken me years to learn about the choices that are out there, and I still don't know everything there is to know. You do not need to understand all the options now; you just need to get a basic understanding of the big three. ***Stocks, bonds and cash are the basic building blocks of good investing***. Most of the list at the top of the page is comprised of these assets; they are just put together in different ways. To build the foundation on which we can anchor our financial future, we are going to get an understanding of the risk/reward profile of each of these three assets. Once we do, we'll know why we need to invest in all of them and perhaps some others, too.

Stocks and the stock market get the most attention from the media, so let's begin with them. Billions of dollars are made or lost every day based on what happens in the stock market. Most people's retirement and investment accounts have at least some stocks in them, so there is a lot of public interest. What is a stock? ***Stocks are ownership in public companies***. Most of the household names with which you are familiar, are public companies. McDonald's, Wal-Mart, Starbucks and Apple Computer are all public companies. Please note that not all companies are public. Mars Inc. for instance, the maker of Peanut M&Ms (my personal favorite) is not public, so we cannot buy their stock.

When we buy even a single share of stock, then we are an owner of that company and have the right to vote for the people who run the company as well as get a share of the profit, but don't let your ego get away from you. To put things into perspective, buying a single share of Starbucks does not give you the right to fire the president of the company, or storm into your local coffee shop, go to the front of the line and demand service because you own the company. As of the writing of this guide, there are well over 593 million shares of Starbucks stock, so your one share equates to ownership of 0.000000168% of the company.

There are two strategies to make money in the stock market. The first is to buy stocks of companies that will increase in value, then sell your shares for a profit. We want to buy shares at a low price and sell them for a higher price. At the same time we need to avoid stocks that decrease in value. If the company you own grows and makes money, their stock price will likely go up. Once you sell those shares of stock you will profit (or lose) the difference between the sales price and the price you originally paid.

Let's look at two monster sized technology companies to show you what happens in the stock market. Assume you bought one share each of Apple Computer and Microsoft at the beginning of 2000 and sold your shares at the end of 2009 (a ten year hold). Look at the table and see how roughly the same dollar amount invested in two different stocks would have worked out for you.

	Purchase Price	Profits Paid	Ending Value*	$ Gain/Loss	% Gain/Loss
Apple	$112.50	$0.00	$842.92	$730.42	649%
Microsoft	$116.56	$10.96	$60.96	-$44.64	-38%

* Apple share split twice, so we ended up selling 4 shares at $210.72 ea.

Microsoft shares split once, so we ended up selling 2 shares at $30.48 ea.

As the table shows, if you bought and held one share of Apple for those 10 years, then you would have made $730 or better than 20% a year. On the other hand, if you bought one share of Microsoft then you would have lost $45, or roughly a 6% loss per year over the same time period. It is clear from the chart that there is big money to be made and lost in the stock market, but the potential is too big to not participate.

The other way to make money with stocks is through company profits. The men and women who run public companies (called the board of directors) decide how much, **if any**, of the profits go to the shareholders. ***Profits are paid to shareholders in the form of dividends***. In most cases, the shareholders get to choose if they want their dividends paid to them in cash or in the form of additional shares of that company's stock. Comparing companies that pay dividends and those that do not, I tend to prefer companies that pay dividends to their shareholders. The reason is that it gives us that extra way to make money on a stock. Even if the share price doesn't move, I will still make some profit on the dividends I receive. If you buy dividend paying stocks, then I strongly recommend you take any dividends in the form of company stock. This will aid in compounding your returns like we learned back in Chapter 1. Once you have stopped working and need more income, take the dividends in cash.

Let me give you an example of how dividends can be an incredible adder to your account. One of the stocks I bought when I was new to the financial services industry was a company called Southern Copper. I was initially attracted to the company because of their high dividend. I invested about $4250 and bought 300 shares of the company's stock at $14.11 per share. The shares are trading today at $32.32. If I sell those 300 shares, I will profit $18.21 ($32.32 − $14.11) per share times 300 shares equals $5463. That's better than a double in 8 years, not too bad. How do dividends help? I have reinvested all my dividends since I first bought the shares, so I actually own 475 shares of the company today. Because of reinvested dividends, the value of **all** my shares of Southern Copper is $15,352 (475 times $32.32). Better than a tripling of my money. That's the power of dividends! That's the power of compounding!

The stock market represents the highest potential returns on our money of the three assets we are discussing in this chapter (stocks, bonds and cash). In fact, from 1950 through 2011, the average annual return for stocks was 10.8%.[iv] That is a pretty good sounding return. When we apply the Rule of 72, we would expect to see our money double every 6 2/3 years. Why wouldn't we put every extra penny into the stock market? The reason is that the stock market moves up and down unpredictably and never in a straight line. During those 62 years, the single best 365 day stretch gave us a 51% gain, but the worst was a loss of 37%.[v] How would you feel if you put $10,000 into the stock market, and a year later your account was worth $6,300? I can tell you from experience that it stinks. Stocks represent one of the highest potential returns, but we subject ourselves to the greatest risk of experiencing losses in our account. What can we do to lessen our risk? Add bonds to our account.

Despite the fact that the stock market is the media favorite, the bond market is about twice the size. Bonds are not as sexy as stocks. They move slower and less dramatically than stocks. *One of the most powerful reasons why we want to add bonds to our account is that they tend to move in the opposite direction of stocks.* When the stock market is going down, our bonds are usually going to be making money. If the stock market is going up, our bonds are likely to lose a little money or break-even. Because of this inverse relationship, adding bonds will smooth out our investment ride (more on this later).

What the heck is a bond anyway? *A bond is an I.O.U. or promise to pay back money.* It is how we as investors are able to lend out our money to a variety of different folks who want to borrow. It gives us great alternatives to finding that desperate concert-going coworker we talked about in Chapter 1. Bonds give us higher paying alternatives to the interest we get paid at a bank or credit union (we will discuss bank and credit union interest below). For example, an older client was not happy with the interest my bank was offering (about 1.25% to lock up her money for two years). Instead of accepting that amount of interest, we decided to buy her a bond paying 4.5% for that same two years.

What determines the interest that a bond pays? There are actually quite a few components that make up the full answer, but for our purposes, let's just focus on two. The two biggest factors are **maturity date** and **credit quality**. **Maturity date** is the precise date that our money will be returned to us. If a bond matures on July 1, then we will get our money back on that date in whatever year is specified. Bonds can be issued for terms as short as 3, 6 or 12 months to as long as 10, 20 or 30 years. All else being equal, the longer the time to maturity the higher the interest rate we will receive. The reason is that if the borrower wants us to wait a long time before we get paid back, then we as investors have more risk that the borrower will not be able to pay us back on the specified maturity date. Therefore, we as lenders will demand the borrower pay us more interest than if we got paid back in a relatively short time period. **Credit quality** is really the same concept as our own credit score we talked about in Chapter 5. More financially secure companies pay less interest to bond holders than weaker companies. That's exactly the same as why people with higher credit scores pay less to borrow than do people with lower scores. Just like lenders have credit agencies to check our scores, bond buyers have agencies that rate the strength of entities that issue bonds.

Why do bonds exist at all? It is how big companies and governments borrow money. If a company or a government does not have or does not want to spend their cash, they can issue bonds as a way to borrow money. Let's say Wal-Mart wants to build another 100 stores that will cost them $400 million. They have three choices; pay cash, sell more company stock or they can choose to issue bonds (borrow the money). If they choose to pay cash, then they would deplete the company reserves substantially. If they issue stock, then each of the existing shares would be worth less (same company value divided by more available shares) Current shareholders typically do not want the value of their existing shares diluted (reduced) because of the company issuing more stock. If the company sells bonds (borrows), they will have to pay interest to bond holders, but they preserve the company's cash, and maintain the value of their existing shares of stock. For these reasons, many companies opt to issue bonds.

Bonds are safer than stocks, but they still have risk. When a company goes out of business or bankrupt, they will stop paying interest on their bonds, and they cannot return the money that you lent them. However, bondholders have a claim to assets that the company does own. Examples of those assets are real estate, vehicles and inventory. Bond holders must be paid in full before a stockholder in a company gets even a penny. While a bondholder in a bankrupt company will likely take a partial loss, it is almost assured that stockholders in that same company will lose their entire investment.

As we just learned, bonds are less risky than stocks because of their slower moving nature and what happens when a company goes out of business. Therefore, we would expect the returns on bonds to be less than stocks (less risk = less reward). History shows us exactly that. Over the same time period noted above (1950 to 2011), bonds have an average annual return of 6.3% (compared to 10.8% for stock), with a best and worst one year performance of +43% and -8%, respectively.[vi] So, does adding this lower performing asset help get us better returns over time? It doesn't, but there are two advantages.

The first advantage is when we create an account with both stocks and bonds; the total account will have substantially less risk of loss than an all stock account. In exchange for a big drop in risk, we only have to give up a relatively small amount of return. To keep this from being a statistics lesson, my wife forced me to move all the math to the end notes and just get to the conclusion. Since a happy wife = a happy life (that equation she does like), I will just tell you that *a half stock half bond portfolio has about 80% of the upside of an all-stock account, but only about half the risk*.[vii]

The second advantage of putting both stock and bonds in our account is that the combination will help us avoid one of the most common mistakes that investors make; emotional decision making. We're going to go into much more detail on this topic in the next chapter. For the time being let's agree that putting both stocks and bonds into our account can be a very good strategy. That leaves us with the last major asset class…cash.

Let's define cash as money in a bank or credit union. ***Cash has no risk of loss***. Cash that is parked in most banks and credit unions is insured and backed by the federal government. In a bank, the insurance on your money comes from the Federal Depository Insurance Corporation (FDIC). I promise you'll see those signs up in virtually every bank you walk into. If you don't see a sign that says in big letters FDIC, then ask an employee there if they are a member of the FDIC. If the answer is no, take your business and your money elsewhere. In a credit union, the insurance is provided by the National Credit Union Insurance Fund (NCUSIF). Same advice applies. Both banks and credit unions have the same insurance limits. In 2014, accounts are insured to $250,000 per individual. As an example, a woman has $200,000 cash on deposit and the bank goes out of business, then the FDIC will refund all her money back. If she has $300,000 on deposit when that same bank fails, then insurance will only return to her $250,000 and $50,000 will be a loss. Since keeping more than the insurance limit in a financial institution is not too likely and because there are ways to increase your insurance that I do not want to detail here; let's agree that cash has no risk of loss. Consequently, the interest rates you will be paid on your cash are relatively low. Since rates can vary between the multiple banks and credit unions, it's hard to nail down historical averages. A very rough estimate of the interest one receives on a savings account over the past 20 years is about 3.25%.[viii]

While you have no risk of losing your money in a bank account, you are subject to another type of risk. Remember when I talked about my experience with bad debt? I compared the amount I owed in 1990 to what that same amount would be in 2014. The fact that prices tend to go up over time is call inflation. ***Purchasing Power risk (inflation) is the risk that your money will not buy the same amount of stuff in the future as it does today***. The historical average of inflation over the same 20 year time period was 2.5%.[ix] So for all intents and purposes, cash in the bank is virtually a break-even proposition (3.25% interest rate − 2.5% inflation = 0.75%). Over time, your money will grow at about the same pace as prices go up. Doesn't sound great, but since you are taking no risk of loss, it makes sense that your rewards are slim. So why would anybody bother to put their money in a savings account if it is only likely to break even? Cash is important to have on hand. Cash is what you use to take care of the unexpected or emergency situations that life tends to throw at you from time to time.

Now we have a basic understanding of the risk and reward tradeoffs for stocks, bonds and cash. Stocks are the most risky, but give us the best potential return. Bonds have less risk than stock and consequently have a lower potential return. Cash has virtually no risk, and therefore, over time the returns on cash are barely more than inflation. All three assets are unique and have a place in our financial future. How much of each we should have depends on a number of factors which we'll take a look at now.

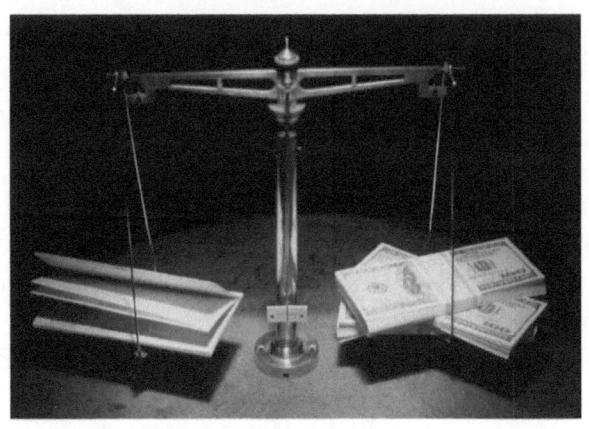

Chapter 10

Stocks, Bonds and Cash: How Much of Each Should We Have?

There is no pat answer to the question posed in the title of this chapter. We know from the last chapter that we need all three. Let's lay down some general guidelines as a starting point. From there we will tweak our asset allocation based on our appetite for risk. ***The term asset allocation is just a fancy way of saying; how much and what kind of stocks, bonds and cash do our accounts hold.*** Consider asset allocation as our overall strategy to win the battle of financial security. Research has shown that 92% of the return on an investment account is driven by asset allocation.[x] Get this piece right and most of the battle is already won. Asset allocation can be applied to a single account or all of our accounts in total. I strongly recommend that you separate your asset allocation by account, because each account should have a specific purpose.

That brings us to the most important element of getting your asset allocation right. The very first question I would ask a prospective client was "what's this money for?" The answer immediately helped me guide the client to an appropriate asset allocation starting point. Generally, *the farther away in time the goal, the greater risk (more stock) the account should have.*

Here are two examples. Example One: a guy in his mid-twenties is starting up an IRA account because his company does not offer a 401K plan. We know from Chapters 7 and 8 that the earliest he's going to use the money is age 59½. With more than 30 years to invest, that person should strongly consider a very heavy weighting of stock, a splash of bonds (sorry, that was a bartending reference from a past life meaning "just a little bit") and no cash. Example Two: a client tells me that she is saving for a down payment on a rental home she plans to buy in 3 years. With only 3 years before her goal, then I would have recommended a maximum of 25% stock, with 60% bonds and 15% in cash. The key point of these two examples: *identifying the goal and its timing are the most important factors in getting the correct asset allocation.* Use the following time-based guidelines for your asset allocation:

	Stocks	Bonds	Cash
Less than 1 year	0%	0%	100%
1 to 3 years	20%	60%	20%
4 to 8 years	30%	60%	10%
9 to 15 years	50%	50%	0%
16 to 25 years	70%	30%	0%
More than 25 years	90%	10%	0%

Looking at the table, there are a couple of takeaways to note. If you are less than a year from using a block of money, then take no risk and put it all in an insured cash account. I dare you to tell me that you are definitely going to use some funds within the year, but you want to get a better return than what risk-free cash is paying. *Take absolutely no risk for short term goals.* If you need the account to grow faster, then your only good option is to save more to make up any expected shortfall. The other takeaway from the table is that if you are saving for a goal that is more than 10 years away, then cash should not be part of your asset allocation (the exception is your emergency fund which we'll talk about shortly). As we learned in the last chapter, cash is a break-even investment. Don't add a virtual 0% interest asset in your account with that much time to invest.

A few of you may be asking, "Should I change my asset allocation as I get closer to actually needing the money?" The answer is absolutely yes. Let's go back to our gal who is saving for the rental house. Suppose she has the good fortune of getting great returns on the stock and bond portions of her account in the first year. If she has made enough for her down payment, then she should go to an all cash asset allocation and start her house hunt. *As you get closer to your goal, you should reduce your risk of loss.*

As with everything in the investing universe, there is always an exception. Your retirement accounts should become less risky as you get closer to retirement. However, keep in mind that the money may have to last several decades after you stop working. Financial planning would be a breeze if we knew the exact day you were going to die. Fortunately, we don't, so plan on living longer than the life expectancy for your gender (yes, women are expected to live longer than men). Unless you have a huge pile of retirement and other savings and/or you have an extremely modest lifestyle, you should always have some risk in your retirement accounts even when you've retired. The reason to keep some riskier assets is that you need to make sure your accounts still grow even though you are withdrawing money from them. Prices will continue to rise (recall inflation from the last chapter), so you need to be able to give yourself raises as prices go up during your retirement years.

Once we understand the goal and timing for an account, the second question I asked a perspective client was whether they had their emergency savings in place. This is essential. *The first block of savings you should build outside your company sponsored or individual retirement account is your emergency fund.* Use the following guidelines to determine how much is adequate for your emergency account.

- Living at home or without housing expenses: 3 times of your typical monthly living expenditures. If you spend about $1,500 per month, then your emergency fund should be $4,000 to $5,000.

- Living under your own roof (either renting or home ownership): 6 times your typical monthly expenses. If you spend $3,000 per month, then your emergency fund should be at least $18,000.

- Within 2 years of or in retirement: 12 times your typical monthly expenditures. If you spend $5,000 per month, then you should have $60,000 in your cash account.

These levels of emergency funding should be adequate to handle more than 90% of life's little surprises. The emergency funds should only be in a cash (savings) account. No Certificate of Deposits (CDs) for your emergency fund. For your information, a CD is an insured bank or credit union product that pays a higher interest rate than a savings account in exchange for your promise to leave the money untouched for a predetermined period of time. The catch on a CD is that it restricts and/or has penalties for withdrawing the funds earlier than agreed. It makes no sense to have restrictions on money that you ultimately do not know on what or when you may need it. I don't want your emergency cash parked in anything that you can't access within 24 hours.

In addition to having the money stashed way for life's curve balls, the emergency fund serves another extraordinarily important function. It should provide you peace of mind to allow your other investment accounts to roll with the inevitable ups and downs of the stock and bond markets. As you may or may not be aware, the stock market crashed in a huge way starting in October of 2007. It hit bottom in March 2009 and was the single worst market we've had since the crash that started in 1929 and led to the Great Depression of the 1930's. During the more recent market crash, people saw their stock accounts get crushed to the tune of 57% over that 18 month period. There was true panic. Let me tell you it was no fun to be a financial advisor during that time. Virtually every inbound phone call was someone who was righteously worried or just plain angry. Those of us in the business did our best to reassure clients (and ourselves) that the world was not coming to an end. We tried to remind clients that the strategies we initially put into place were still valid and viable long term approaches to investing. Those with ample savings outside of the investment accounts (aka emergency funds) were far more likely to heed our advice and stay invested. Those who did not have substantial cash savings were for the most part inconsolable. They allowed their honest emotions to lead them to do exactly the wrong thing at the wrong time.

As a financial advisor, when I went through all the pros and cons of a particular investment or strategy, part of the conversation always revolved around trusting their gut. I told every potential client or young person I met to trust their gut. Whether we like it or not, most of us have a great built in sense to know whether the person we're dealing with is full of crap or giving it to us straight up. My exact quote was; "If you even have the faintest inkling that I am full of it, then please trust your gut and find another advisor. Ultimately you are going to be doing both of us a favor by taking your business elsewhere." Not the best line for a salesperson I'll admit, but it's true. Your gut is right 99% of the time. *The most notable exception is when it comes to timing investments. For these decisions, don't trust your gut!!!*

Emotional investing will ultimately cause you to make poor decisions. The reason being is that the only time it feels good to invest is when all the news is good and you see all the money that other people are making in the markets; you want in. Sorry to tell you that you are too late to the party, and in all likelihood, you are investing at or near a market top. Conversely, when the market is getting beaten up (which it does periodically), you get investment statements that keep showing a lower value than the previous one. You ultimately reach a point where you're sick of seeing another down statement. That's when you say to yourself, "Forget this…I just need to protect what I have left." You pull the trigger and sell your stocks. Congratulations, you just bought at a market top and sold at a market low. This happens with each and every market cycle. People are emotional beings and emotions will invariably lead you astray when it comes to timing investment decisions.

In reality we need to do the opposite of what our gut tells us in the investment realm. A very famous investor named Warren Buffet wrote an opinion piece published in the New York Times on October 18th 2008 (in the middle of the more recent market crash), "Be fearful when others are greedy, and be greedy when others are fearful." Another quote I love, credited to Joe Kennedy in 1928 (just months before the biggest market crash in modern times), "You know it's time to sell when the shoeshine boy give you stock tips…" In other words, when everybody is rushing into the stock market, it is probably time to take some profits, and when everybody is getting out of the market, it may be time to do some bargain-hunter buying. If you ever want to use your gut feelings to time an investment decision, then just do the opposite.

While you must avoid making emotional decisions on timing your investments, you do need to embrace how you are wired to handle market fluctuation. ***Never take on more risk than you can handle regardless of what the time based guidelines indicate***. I am extremely risk tolerant. During the 2008 meltdown, my long term accounts were down 50% or more. I never strayed from my strategy. In fact, as the market got closer to the bottom, I began to add additional stock (per Mr. Buffet's advice). There are very few rookie or novice investors who can tolerate the same level of account fluctuations that I experienced. **Start more conservatively than you believe you are**, and once you've gone through a couple of market cycles without changing your investments, then consider changing to a more aggressive asset allocation with a larger percentage of stock. For long term accounts, the 50/50 stock bond portfolio is a great way to start investing.

Take a look at the graphs on the next page. They show four different asset allocations over a 4-year time period:[xi] There are a three items we need to take away from our review of the graphs. 1) Note the roughness of each line showing the value of each asset allocation over time. More stock in the asset allocation means the ride is going to be very bumpy. Less stock in the asset allocation gives you a relatively smooth ride. 2) Recall the discussion in the last chapter about the relationship between risk and reward. During the time period shown, note that the asset allocations with more stock performed better (+76% average increase for the aggressive and the all stock asset allocations) compared to the allocations with less stock (+35% average increase for low risk and for the moderate risk asset allocations). 3) Carefully look at the first parts of each of the charts. From the start date to the market bottom on March 9th, 2009 the most conservative account lost 2.5% in 4 months, while the all stock account lost 18%. Before you just say to yourself that you want the asset allocation with the best performance, ask yourself if you would be ok with losing 1 out of every five dollars you invested in the first four months of investing (like what happened to the all-stock portfolio). Do not make this an ego issue. Trust your gut to pick which line has the smoothness with which you would be comfortable. With these three items in mind, let's take a look at the graphs on the next page.

The bottom line is that you should use time to base your asset allocation. Temper the allocation with your risk tolerance. Do not try to guess or use your emotions as a guide to change your strategy. Timing the market is a losing game because your emotions will invariably cause you to make bad decisions. Stick with your asset allocation except under the following two circumstances. As we already learned, make your asset allocation more conservative as you get closer in time to using the money. The only other time you change your asset allocation is if your goal for the account changes. Let's say that you decide to use money that you had earmarked for long term savings to purchase an apartment building instead. Since the goal for that block of money has changed from long term to immediate, then take all the risk off that block of funds. You do not want to experience a substantial loss just prior to using the money. ***Do not change your strategy unless the goal for the account changes. If the goal and timing has not changed, then don't change your asset allocation.*** If you stick to these basics then you'll win the battle of achieving financial security. Now let's look at the many different ways to implement your asset allocation strategy.

Chapter 11

Implementing Your Asset Allocation Strategy

As of the writing this guidebook there are tens of thousands of publicly traded stocks and bonds in the world, so how do we pick the right ones? My initial response is to tell you not to buy any individual stocks or bonds at all. Now before you throw your hands up in disgust or toss this book into the trash, please give me a chance to explain. We've already talked about taking the right amount of risk. When it comes to picking stocks and bonds, we can lower our risk of loss by investing in multiple companies covering different industries instead of just picking a few. Here's how it works. Suppose you own stock from only 2 companies and one goes out of business, you might lose half your money invested in stocks. If you own 20 stocks and one goes to zero, then you might lose 5%. If you own 100 stocks, then you might be down 1%. In the financial service business, we use the term diversification. ***Diversification is spreading the risk in your account over many different assets (stocks and/or bonds).*** It's really just a fancy way of saying, "don't put all your eggs in one basket."

One of the most common mistakes I saw when reviewing customer's accounts was over-concentration of a single company or industry. It makes total sense when you consider the emotional side we all have. People like to invest in industries with which they are familiar. Doctors tended to own too many healthcare and drug companies. Engineers were invariably over allocated to technology. Employees of companies who offer a stock purchase plan tended to have too much of their own company's stock. This is a critical error. ***Never put yourself in a situation where your income, insurance benefits, retirement and personal wealth are tied to the fortunes of a single company***. For those of you who don't believe me, do another internet search on a defunct company named Enron. Most of Enron's employees were financially wiped out and learned the hard way the lesson of diversification.

When we are talking about buying a basket of stocks, not only do we want to give ourselves exposure to many industries, but we also need to get all different size companies in our account. Most of the stock examples used so far in this book have been examples of giant American companies. Our accounts should hold medium and small company stock as well. Within the investment arena, I like to divide the stock market into the following five sections. For your information, the term "Cap" shown below is short for capitalization meaning the value or size of the company:

- **US Large Cap**: These are the biggest American companies which are well established and typically have stable businesses. The stock prices of the largest companies tend to move more slowly than their smaller counterparts. US large Cap should be the foundation of our stock holdings. On top of that foundation, we are going to add more stocks from the following four categories.

- **US Mid Cap**: These are big companies, but not necessarily as well known as the giants. An example is Petsmart, Inc., a national chain of retail stores catering to pets. We want mid cap stocks in our account because if they can grow into a Large Cap company, we are going to make a lot of money by owning their stock.

- **US Small Cap**: These are smaller companies that tend to be more regional in nature. Examples with which you may be familiar are Brunswick Corp, most recognizable for their bowling equipment and Coinstar whose machines allow customers to dump a jar of coins into a box and turn it into easily spendable cash without having to count it. Use the same logic to add these to our account as we did for the mid-caps. If these companies can grow into international leaders we'll make a fortune on their stock. Unfortunately, most will never make it and many will go out of business. So while they represent the greatest potential of the US stocks, that potential comes at the expense of additional risk of loss.

- **Developed International**: These are the bigger non-American companies from the most stable countries in Western Europe, the UK, Japan and Australia. Many should be familiar to you; Toyota, Nestle, British Petroleum (BP) to name a few. These types of stocks should be part of our account because we live in an era of global corporations and a global economy. If we only have US stock, we are limiting the potential of our total stock holdings and ignoring the concept of diversification.

- **Emerging Markets**: This is the wild west of stock investing. Companies in the emerging markets primarily include those from Brazil, Russia, India and China as well as others from all over the rest of the globe. Because the companies in the emerging markets are from countries with less established economies and are subject to political crackdowns and/or public unrest we need to be wary of holding too many of these stocks.

In general, the smaller company stock has more risk (and therefore the greater the potential return) than the medium and large companies. Similarly, the emerging markets can wildly outperform and underperform their developed international counterparts.

There are hundreds of US large caps and thousands of stocks from each of the other categories. That makes selecting the right ones a potentially overwhelming task and was the basis for my advice at the beginning of the chapter to not buy any individual stocks. There are two products that do that job for us. *They are called mutual funds and exchange traded funds.* We are going to discuss these later, but before we go to that topic, I do want to give some important advice to those of you who choose to pick some of your own stocks.

First and foremost, the stock market is the biggest casino on the planet. If you have a passion for playing the game, then do it with some ground rules. If you don't have a passion for it, don't play yourself; let professionals do it for you through the products I just mentioned. For those of you who want to play, here are the three rules you should follow to insure you have a rational rather than emotional approach to the stock market.

Rule 1: Know why you are buying the stock. Is the company launching a new product? Do you see them dominating their industry? Are they going to be bought out by a larger player? Do they pay a big dividend? Whatever the reason, know why you think the company's business or stock price is going to go up. If you can't explain precisely why you want to buy a stock, it's probably not a good choice. A friend, or neighbor with a hot tip does not qualify as a good reason to buy a stock.

Rule 2: Before you buy the stock, know your profitability goal. Are you going to sell once you're up 10%, 50% or

200%? Most stock players do not establish a sell discipline before they buy. They watch their stock climb and get greedy (another pesky emotion that can sabotage us). They want to squeeze another couple of dollars per share from their pick. Too many times, the stock price will drop down back to where they bought it or below. Their gut told them to hold on because they want every dime out of their good idea. Let me tell you that no one knows when a stock is going to change direction. Here's a phrase I use on a regular basis, "never bitch about a winner!" If you make money on a stock idea, congratulate yourself and move onto the next. Never play the "what if" game, stick to your discipline.

Rule 3: Know your threshold for pain. Just like we set goals on the upside, we have to establish a maximum loss amount **before** we buy a stock. If the reason why we bought the stock (Rule 1) is wrong, how much are will willing to lose before we cut our losses and run. This is yet another emotional trap. People hate to admit they're wrong. Selling a loser stock is an acknowledgement that we made a bad decision. Investors tend to use the logic, "the stock will come back if I just hold onto it." This rationale can wipe you out. Before I became a professional in this business, I bought a stock without the discipline. I bought a 100 shares stock at $34/share and it went up for a couple weeks, then turned around and started to move down. It fell all the way to $2/share and never came back. I finally sold it for $1.87/share losing $3200 after holding on to it for over 10 years. As you can see, not having the sell discipline can be rather costly. For the stock pickers amongst you, follow these three rules and you will increase your odds of good outcomes.

Whether we choose to pick individual stocks or buy mutual funds/exchange traded funds, we must stay diversified. If we chose the mutual fund/exchange traded fund, they can give us a very easy way to stay diversified without any effort on our part. Before we detail these products, we need to understand the same diversification concept with our bond holdings.

Just like the stock markets, let's break down the bond market into smaller pieces so we can understand the broad categories into which we need to have exposure. The first three on the list to follow (government, mortgage-backed and investment grade) should make up the lion's share of our bond holdings. With those as our base, we will sprinkle some from the last three on the list (High-yield, International Treasuries, and International Corporates).

- **US Government Bonds**: These are bonds that are direct obligations of the US government. They are paid by the taxes we pay and other federal revenue. There are a large variety of government bonds with different maturities and other characteristics. The scope of this guidebook prohibits me from going into every type, thank goodness. Generally speaking, US government bonds are considered to be risk free. The reasons are that the US political system is very stable, the US is currently the largest economy on the planet and if the government ever ran out of money, they could just print more cash to pay off their outstanding bonds. Because of their status as being risk free, government bonds pay us a relatively low interest. This is similar to the concept of our insured savings accounts.

- **Mortgage Backed Bonds**: Recall when we talked about good debt in Chapter 4. Most people need to borrow large sums of money to buy real estate. These mortgages are sold by the banks to an agency which bundles them together to be the collateral for bonds the agency sells. These bonds tend to be very secure because they're backed by the properties upon which the mortgage was taken. Since real estate is subject to ups and downs like the stock market, they carry more risk than government bonds and therefore pay us more interest.

- **Corporate Bonds**:
    - o **Investment Grade**: These are bonds that are issued by the stronger US companies. As we learned from Chapter 9, companies often opt to issue bonds (borrow) rather than using their cash or selling company stock. While the risk of an investment grade bond defaulting (not paying back the money borrowed) is low, they are more risky than mortgage backed or government bonds. Depending on the credit worthiness of the issuing company they will pay considerably more interest than either of the first two.

    - o **High Yield**: Before many of you were even alive, these types of bonds were called **Junk Bonds**. As the old name implies, they bare considerable risk that the issuing company will not be able to pay back their bonds. Just like the emerging markets is the wild west of stock investing, High Yield is the rocket fuel of the US bond market. High yield bonds pay investors potentially very high stock market-like rates of return, so we definitely want a sprinkling of them as part of our bond exposure inside our account.

- **International Bonds**: International bonds have an extra component of risk and reward that US bonds do not have. The added characteristic is that they pay us in local currency (British Bonds pay in Pounds, Japanese Bonds pay in the Yen). If we choose wisely, we can make extra money when we exchange the local currency into US dollars. I break down international bonds into two broad categories
    - o **International Treasuries**: Governments around the globe need to borrow money, and depending on the stability of the country, these

can be a good addition to our bond holdings. The reason is that some of these foreign treasuries are very safe like US treasuries, but they offer significantly higher interest rates.

o **International Corporates**: For the same reasons we want international exposure in our stock investments, we definitely want to have the same diversification within our bonds. Strong foreign companies deserve our attention when we are diversifying our bond account.

Here is the problem when we talk about diversifying our bonds. Most bonds are issued with a face value of $1,000/each. Particularly when we are just making our way into investment world, we may have just one or two thousand dollars in total. *With limited funds, it is impossible to create a diversified bond account buying individual bonds*. If your chosen asset allocation from the last chapter includes bonds, we simply can't ignore this important asset type. The solution is to get your diversified account using mutual funds and/or exchange traded funds.

Mutual Funds (MFs) and Exchange Traded Funds (ETFs) are the most common and easiest way to create a diversified asset allocation with limited funds. They are not just for small investors. Million dollar accounts hold MFs and ETFs because they relieve the investor of the responsibility of having to decide which stocks and bonds they ought to buy. With thousands of stocks and bonds to choose from, it's often better to delegate that responsibility to people whose only job is to pick assets for us.

Here's how these products are structured. Investors (you and I) buy shares of MFs and ETFs. Our money is pooled together with other investors who have also bought the same fund. Because the money from thousands of investors is combined, the folks running the MFs or ETFs can create a diversified account for the whole group of investors who bought shares in the fund. For example, I own a fund that targets Global Large Cap stocks. At the time of writing, the fund trades at roughly $37 per share, but owns 81 different stocks. For every dollars I invest, I am actually buying fractional shares in 81 different stocks. That would be impossible for me to do directly in the stock market. Another fund I own in a retirement account holds literally hundreds of different stocks and thousands of different bonds. *Using Mutual Funds and Exchange Traded funds is a great way to execute an asset allocation strategy regardless of the amount of money to be invested.*

I am a huge proponent of the complete asset allocation types of these two products. These are funds that combine both stocks and bonds in a single investment. If you are one of the majority who does not want to spend most of their day following individual stocks and bonds, then let someone else do it for you. "Set and forget" can ultimately be the best approach to long term investing. By doing this, our only job is to maintain our savings discipline (regularly adding to our accounts) and we hand off the rest.

Why do both mutual funds and exchange traded funds exist? There are many differences between the two. For our purposes, let's highlight just a few now. Before I detail the most important differences, we need to understand what an index is. *An index is simply a way to measure the performance of an entire market or just a particular piece of it.* Lots of different indexes are published for both the stock and bond markets. Two of the most common ones for the US markets are the Standard and Poor's 500 (S&P 500) which measures the performance of the 500 largest US public companies and the Barclay's Aggregate which is a broad US bond index. All funds are judged against these or other indexes. With that in mind, the first major difference between the two types of funds is managed vs. non-managed. **Mutual Funds have a dedicated portfolio manager** or managers who execute the buy and sell of stocks and bonds based on a

72

variety of objective and subjective criteria. **The Exchange Traded Fund is not managed with any subjectivity at all**. The criteria for picking assets going into an ETF are predetermined by a computerized formula. These formulas are built to replicate the variety of stock and bond indexes that are publicly available. The advantage of the human element is that they can possibly outperform an index with superior asset selection (stock and bond picking). The exchange traded fund will never beat its index because it is built to mirror it. In fact, the ETF will slightly underperform its index because every ETF has an internal cost (called an expense ratio) for running and marketing the fund.

That fact leads us to the second major difference. ***Wall Street always pays itself first***. No matter how well or poorly your investments perform, somebody is making money off your account. When you compare the two types of funds, mutual funds are almost always more expensive than an equivalent ETFs. Expense ratios vary widely among funds. The lowest cost EFT I've seen has an expense ratio of 0.07 of one percent annual expenses for a fund mirroring the S&P 500. That means for every $1000 you have invested in this ETF, the fund company charges you 70 cents per year. Compare that to the expense ratio of the Global Large Cap fund I own which has an expense ratio of 0.89%, or $8.90 per $1000 invested. That's a huge difference, so why would you even consider the mutual fund?

A mutual fund has breaks. By that, I mean that if the manager sees trouble coming to the markets, she can lower the portfolio's risk by picking safer or fewer stocks and/or moving money into bonds or cash which will not go down with the stock market. The ETF has no breaks...as the market goes so does your account value. Additionally, the mutual fund manager can outperform her index. For example, let's suppose an index is up 10% for a year, but the mutual fund was up 13% because of superior stock picking. We would be better off paying the higher expense ratio and netting 12.11% (13% less 0.89% expenses) compared to 9.93% that the ETF retuned (10% less 0.07% expenses). On the other hand, if the fund manager matches the index or underperforms, then the investor pays more and gets less return. The matter of which is better is open to debate. I own both types of funds, so I'll leave the choice to you. Just be aware that all investments involve some level of cost no matter what anyone tells you. There are no free lunches on Wall Street, more on that in the next chapter.

To finish off this chapter, I want to talk about an investment type that is very good for your retirement accounts. They are available as mutual funds and as ETFs. Most of the company sponsored retirement plans now have these options. It is how I invest in my current and past two 401K plans. They are called "target date" funds. Their fund names usually include a calendar year like 2020 or 2055. These are fully diversified asset allocation funds. All you do is pick the fund that has the year closest to when you plan to retire. If you are age 30 in 2015 and want to retire at age 65, then select the 2050 Fund. Once you pick it, you're done, the fund does the rest. It will systematically reduce your risk as you get closer to your target year (like we talked about in Chapter 10). When you are 30+ years from retiring, the fund will be almost entirely stocks with a bias towards more risky stock types. Over time, the fund will morph itself to become more conservative to where the asset allocation will end up roughly 25% stock, 50% bonds and 25% cash when you hit the target date. If you decided that you are either more risk tolerant or risk adverse than most, then just choose the fund with a closer date to be more conservative or a farther date to be more aggressive.

We now have a basic understanding implementing an asset allocation via a diversified blend of individual stocks and bonds, through funds or potentially a combination of all of them. I enjoy the world's largest casino. I play individual stocks to supplement my overall asset allocation strategy. Be advised that I was a professional, and still 70% of my total investments are mutual funds and exchange traded funds. If you're going to play the markets, too, then make sure you have the majority of your investments in funds that are not subject to the perils of emotional investing. The advice I gave my clients was to play the individual stock game with not more than 10% of their account value. The last major question we need to address is whether we can do it ourselves, or do we need to have the help of a professional.

Chapter 12

The Costs of Investing: Go it Alone or Pay for Help?

As was mentioned in the prior chapter; investing always costs money. There can be upfront costs like commissions to buy products, embedded management fees (like the expense ratios of funds we discussed) or both. The goal of this chapter is to give you the confidence to manage your own investments until you have amassed well over $250,000 and/or you are nearing retirement. The reason why we want to consider enlisting help once we have over a quarter of a million dollars is that we may want to add some other asset classes beyond the standard stock, bond and cash threesome. Some of these other types of investments (which we'll talk about in the next chapter) can have substantial minimum investments and overall wealth requirements. The reason for the retirement exception to going it alone is that as we approach retirement, we'll need to create a spending plan rather than a savings plan which can be substantially more complex. As part of that spending plan, it may be in your best interest to buy a product that provides guaranteed lifetime income. These guaranteed products will require you to engage the services of a licensed person.

Since it is quite likely that I have found you a few dollars short of 250,000 and a couple years younger than retirement age, let's decide whether it's worth paying someone to assist you with your investing. *Your overall philosophy about where to invest should embrace the fact that the less you spend on sales commissions and embedded costs, the more money you get to keep for yourself.* The cost of investing tends to be proportional to the service level provided. Self service firms and mail-in/internet providers are the least expensive by far. Financial service firms (including insurance agencies) with offices where you can sit and plan with a licensed broker are more expensive. There are also alternatives in the middle. Let's start with the least expensive because these are the ones to use if I can convince you to manage your own investments. A company called Vanguard is probably the lowest cost provider. They offer a wide variety of no-load mutual funds. The term "no-load" means that there is no commission to buy their mutual funds. They also have a similarly large variety of low/no commission ETFs. The internal cost of their funds (expense ratios of both the ETFs and MFs) are extremely low. Vanguard's $20 annual account fee is waived if you agree to get your statements and other documents via the internet or have an account value greater than $10,000 for a mutual fund account or $50,000 for a brokerage (ETF, stock and bond) account. The downside of using Vanguard is that as a new (low dollar) investor you are not going to get a lot of help, nor are you going to be able to sit down and speak face-to-face with a representative. Account set-up and maintenance is accomplished through the phone, internet and via snail mail.

Another low cost provider is Fidelity Investments. As of the writing of this guide, they have no account opening or annual maintenance fees. Like Vanguard, they offer no-load mutual funds and low/no cost EFT trades. They both have funds that allow us to pick a single fund that will match an asset allocation for our specific goal. The downside of Fidelity funds is that their expense ratios are higher than you will experience with the average Vanguard fund. Both fund companies offer a 2050 retirement fund. Currently,

Vanguard's expense ratio is 0.19% vs. Fidelity's at 0.77%. This means that on an annual basis, investing in Fidelity's 2050 fund is four times more expensive than the equivalent Vanguard fund. Everything else being equal, paying four times the fee for 30 to 40 years can certainly impact your end result. Fidelity does have the advantage that they have a physical presence in many metro areas around the country. When you are setting up your accounts you have the option to sit down with an advisor and get help opening your account and selecting a fund or funds that are appropriate. Both firms will allow you to make stock trades for about $7.50 per trade (please visit both firm's websites for the details). [xii]

Moving into the middle tier on the cost-service continuum, we come to Charles Schwab (as the best example). Schwab offers no fee accounts, physical locations, no load funds, a handful of low cost ETFs and reasonable commission rates for stock, bond and ETF trades. The downside of Schwab is that their sales model is geared to putting your money into fee based accounts. The "fee based" account is the direction that the whole industry is moving. The way these accounts work is that for an ongoing management fee, Schwab and most others will actively trade your account for you. The back office think-tank will tweak your asset allocation to try to drive your returns higher than a static asset allocation model would provide. During my years in the business, I became skeptical about whether this type of active management would consistently generate enough extra return to justify the additional ongoing cost. Fee based accounts aside, Schwab is a reputable firm and if you did want a more hands on customer service experience, this firm can provide that to you.

At the high end of the cost spectrum you will find banks, insurance agencies and full service brokerages. Fees can be higher, costs to buy and sell stocks, bonds and ETFs are higher. Since these companies are sales revenue driven organizations, you will not find any no-load mutual funds. While this gives you a lot more options to choose from, the cost for a "loaded" mutual fund purchase can range from 4.5% to 5.75% for any purchases less than $50,000. If I wanted to by $10,000 of the loaded XYZ Fund, then it would cost me $450 to $575. Right off the bat my account is down about 5% before my money even gets invested. So why would anyone opt for this level of cost? There are two possibilities; 1) they don't know any better, or 2) they need or want a dedicated advisor and are willing to pay for personalized advice. There is nothing wrong with taking this path. If you have zero interest in investing or your life and career just do not allow for the time to manage the investment part of your personal finance, then pay for the service. Providing this service is how I made my living for quite some time. If you do choose to use an advisor, then the most important thing is to pick the right one.

Which full-service company you pick is not important. Picking an honest advisor is crucial. Unfortunately, there are lots of advisors out there that simply do not give a darn about your financial future. In my opinion, ***most*** financial advisors are not worth the money you pay them. They only care about themselves. There is a term in the industry called Y-T-B or yield-to-broker. Unscrupulous advisors only care about how much money they make on a sale. In fact, it is the first question many ask when learning about a financial product. We need to be aware of these men and women and stay away. This is where we want to trust our gut. If you have even the faintest inkling that you are not getting the full straight scoop from an advisor, get the heck out of there without signing a thing. When you do find a full service advisor you trust, ask this question, "How are you being paid for this product or service?" It is a fair question that deserves an honest answer. Are they making a one-time upfront commission and does that commission come out of our initial investment amount (like a loaded mutual fund)? Are there ongoing charges paid to the advisor (aka "trailers" like we see in fee-based accounts)? In our lives outside of the personal finance world, we would never buy anything without knowing what it costs, so why should financial products and services be different? If an advisor is evasive or throws out the response, "it costs you nothing," then you are probably with the wrong advisor. One caveat, there are products offered by full service brokerages that do not have any up-front fees, but trust me, there is always a catch. The catch is usually either a very high annual expense ratio or a substantial penalty for selling the product in the first several years of ownership. Find out what the expenses and/or the other catches are, so you can make a fully informed decision. Remember, it is your money that's paying the fees, so understand what you're getting before you buy it.

We've covered a lot of ground in this chapter, but let's boil it down to a couple of key points to remember. 1) The cost of investing is more or less proportional to the level of service provided by the firms. 2) The lower the cost of investing, the better off you'll be over the long haul. 3) Higher level service firms are pushing managed accounts. Whether paying for this management is in your best interests is yet to be proven. 4) Those of us choosing to pay higher investment costs should be certain we are dealing with a reputable individual regardless of what firm they're associated with. Understand these four points and you'll be able to make a good decision on whether to go it alone or pay for advice. The last point we need to cover on investing is how we manage our accounts once they've been established.

Chapter 13

Account Maintenance and Add-ons

The account is opened. The asset allocation is set to match your goal and risk tolerance. The automatic ongoing contribution is established. What now? There are just two things you need to do at this point: periodic reviews and rebalancing. Reviewing your account is simple. Actually look at your investment statement. Sounds simple enough, but I can't tell you how many people simply pay no attention to their investments. On the first page, check out your account value. Keep track of the progress you're making. We know that not every statement is going to show an increase in value even if we're adding more money. The ups and downs of the markets that we learned about in Chapter 9 will prevent our account from going up every time, but be familiar with the movement your account experiences. If you decide that the swings on your statement are too large then make your account more conservative by raising the percentage of bonds or cash (Chapter 10). As a reminder, never sell out of your stocks completely. If you do, then you've fallen into the emotional investing trap. If you're scared about your account, the economy or the markets, it's probably a good time to add extra money to the account. There is absolutely no reason to look at your investments more than once a month, the ups and downs can and probably will drive you nuts.

In addition to noting the account value, spend two minutes making sure the new money is being credited to your account and it's being invested as you instructed. You should receive monthly statements if you have a regular contribution and purchase. You may only get statements four times per year if there is no purchase activity. Recalling Chapter 2, *please make that regular ongoing contribution.* By doing so, you are effectively executing a sound investment strategy called "dollar cost averaging."

Dollar cost averaging is a strategy of making fixed dollar purchases over an extended period of time. In a volatile market place, it allows the investor to buy more shares when share prices are low and fewer when prices are high. Investors using this strategy will have an average cost per share lower than the average share price over the same period of time. Look at the table below which illustrates an investor who buys $100 of a no-load fund mutual fund once per month.

	Share Price	$100/mo. Shares
January	$ 49.90	2.004008
February	$ 51.40	1.945525
March	$ 50.97	1.961938
April	$ 45.34	2.205558
May	$ 38.43	2.602134
June	$ 39.95	2.503129
July	$ 40.48	2.470356
August	$ 40.73	2.455193
September	$ 38.95	2.567394
October	$ 34.65	2.886003
November	$ 46.44	2.153316
December	$ 42.10	2.375297
Total Shares	n/a	28.12985
Average	$ 43.28	$ 42.66

There are two items to note. First, the investor buys more shares for his $100 in months with lower prices (May and October) than he does when the prices are higher (February and March). Also note at the bottom of the table how his average cost per share is lower than the average share price over the entire year. A lower cost per share is always a good outcome, so invest consistently throughout the year.

All that is left to do for account maintenance is to rebalance. **Rebalancing is the regular process of returning your portfolio to the same asset allocation with which you started.** Over time, assets will perform differently. If you do no maintenance on your account, then you will end up with a different asset allocation than your goal and risk tolerance dictated. Here is how the process works; assume you start with a 50/50 stock to bond asset allocation for our account:

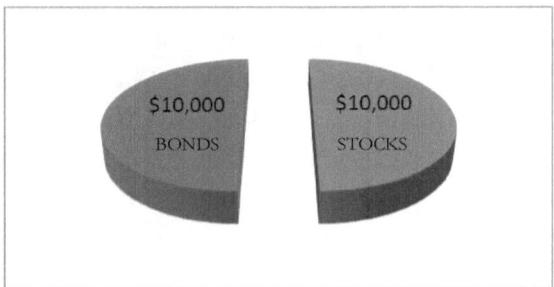

Suppose after a year when the stock market boomed and the bond market suffered, your account might look like this:

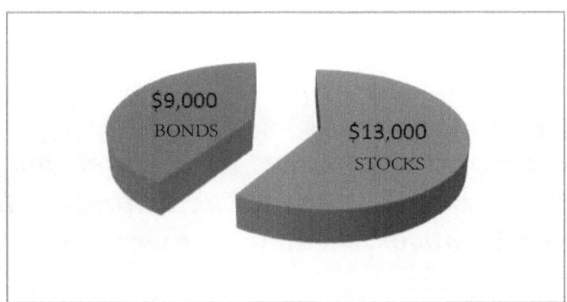

The account made great money for the year (up $2,000 on $20,000 invested or +10%), but your account now has a ratio of about 60% stocks to 40% bonds. This asset allocation will be significantly more volatile than the one you initially chose. In order to bring you back to what was originally established, you will rebalance your account. You need to sell some of your stock and use that money to buy bonds. In our example, you will sell $2,000 of stock and buy $2,000 in bonds which will return us to our desired 50/50 asset allocation.

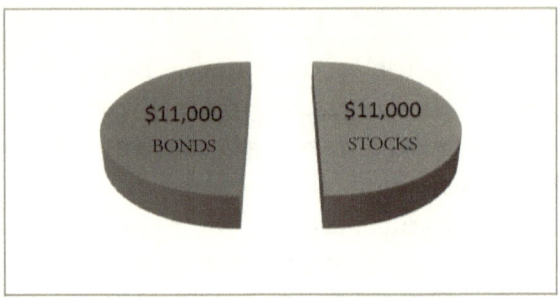

One of the greatest aspects of rebalancing is that it forces us to do the right thing at the right time. Think about the example we just went through. We had a great year in the stock market. Stocks were up 30%. The bond market was down 10%. By rebalancing we were forced to take profits on the stock portion (we sold high) and used that money to buy more bonds (we bought low). This is exactly what we are supposed to do, but emotionally, it is difficult to either sell an asset that's running up or add money to an asset that lost us money the prior year. In order to completely remove the emotions from the process, establish a fixed time to rebalance during the year. Once or twice a year is sufficient for our retirement accounts. Because of tax rules, we'll rebalance our taxable accounts (non-IRA/401K) every 366 days (1 year + 1 day). Here is a final note on rebalancing. *If we pick a single fund that accomplishes our total asset allocation (a comfortable mix of both stocks and bonds), then we do not need to rebalance*. The fund manager will do that for us. The manager will have the luxury of using new fund purchases and other cash flows to accomplish rebalancing throughout the year.

*****

As you grow your wealth, you may want to consider adding other assets to your accounts. The following is a partial list of other assets that you may want to add to your total portfolio. Use caution that you don't place too big a bet on any of these alternative assets. They can be more risky than stocks, but the returns can be oversized as well.

Real Estate: I know we went through this in some detail in Chapter 4, but I want to remind you. You do not need to confine your thinking to single family homes. You can invest in commercial, farm land, industrial, office or multi-unit apartments. There are some great tax advantages to owning income property, and don't forget about the income stream that these assets can generate. The downsides of real estate can be many. Unexpected repairs and maintenance costs, taxes, insurance, unoccupied units (lost rent) as well as dealing with tenants can be a nightmare. People can pay late, not pay at all, or trash your property. One idea to keep in mind if you take this path is that receiving less rent for a problem free tenant is absolutely worth it. In the context of the stock market, there are a number of "stocks" you can buy that are actually real estate investment trusts (REITs). These securities will vastly simplify your exposure to Real Estate, but they do not carry the same tax benefits of direct property ownership.

Precious Metals: Throughout most of human history, gold and silver (and many others) have been valued. Today is no different. If you want to purchase precious metals, make sure that they represent not more than 5% of your total net worth. You can buy special securities on the stock market called Exchange Traded Notes that are backed by the actual physical metal. For example, symbol GLD (you can look this up online if you're interested) represents $1/10^{th}$ of an ounce of gold. It trades just like a stock, so the shares are extremely liquid (you can buy or sell anytime the stock market is open). If you actually want to buy and store the physical metal, then buy United States minted coins. These are easily tradable in any coin or gold shop. If you buy foreign coins or bars, then in most cases, a dealer will need to melt down the coins or bars to verify the quantity and grade of the metal. It's probably not worth the time and cost to store physical metal no matter how cool it seems.

Commodities: The world eats and builds using agricultural and industrial commodities. Examples are coffee, wheat and soybeans on the agricultural side, and crude oil, copper and iron on the industrial side. Enormous profits and losses can be made in an extremely short period of time. Commodities are traded using an instrument called Futures Contracts. These contracts use leverage which allows the contract holder to put up a relatively small amount of money to control a large basket of a particular commodity. For example, a coffee futures contract represents 37,500 lbs. of coffee beans, but might only require the investor to put up $5,000. Currently, regular coffee costs about $8/lb. at the market, so an investor controls $300,000 worth of coffee but only risks $5,000. Because assets are traded with all that leverage, even small price movements can wipe you out or make you rich. If you are going to add these types of assets to your holdings, pay a professional commodity trader to do this on your behalf.

Stock Options: Similar to commodities, investors can choose to invest in stock options which allow you to use leverage to control a large block of stock. Options can be used to speculate (gamble) or hedge a position in your stock account (buy insurance). Options allow an investor to profit (or lose) regardless of the direction a stock moves. There are countless strategies to employ using stock options, and the scope of this guide simply does not allow us to go into the myriad possibilities. Stock options are mentioned here, so you know they exist. Once you have some experience in the stock market, then do a little additional research on the topic and see if they may be something you want to add to your account.

Hedge Funds: Hedge funds are the black box of all the alternative assets you can add to your account. The reason why they are so mysterious is that hedge funds employ a multitude of different strategies which fund managers are not required to publish on a frequent basis. Some hedge funds strategies include currency trading, merger arbitrage, market neutral price inefficiencies, market shorting, and private equity. I'm not going to waste your time to explain what each of these is. The bottom line for hedge funds is that you need to be an accredited investor to play in this game. Current regulations of the Securities and Exchange Commission (SEC) define an accredited investor as one who has over a $1,000,000 net worth excluding their first home and/or one who has made $250,000 a year for the past two years. This book has likely found you a few dollars short of those limits, but file this asset type in the back of your brain. The time may come when you do want to place some of your investment capital in these alternatives. The key to remember on hedge fund investments is that they tend to be very illiquid, meaning that you cannot get your money out when you choose. Rather, there are very few narrow windows during the year where your money becomes available to withdraw.

*****

That pretty much covers all the basics of building wealth from creating a saving discipline all the way to investing your assets. If any of the investing topics really grabbed you, then I encourage you to do more research on them. Since I'm not an avid reader, I'm not going to make any specific book recommendations, but search the internet and the bookstore for the specific topics that inspire you. For general resources, start with two internet sites; finance.yahoo.com and investopedia.com. Both sites are great places to start learning more. The following chapters are a couple of topics that came up frequently during my years of financial advising, but did not neatly flow in the logical progression I tried to present in the preceding chapters. Please read on to grab some useful advice and information on insurance and home buying.

Chapter 14

Life and Health Insurance

Life insurance is a useful tool to protect your family in case you die during your working years. ***Buy life insurance to cover the financial responsibilities you have***. This product is a contract between you and an insurance company. The insurance company agrees to pay a death benefit to whomever you specify in exchange for you paying regular premiums. In my family's case, we chose to get enough coverage to pay off our family house, cover college expenses and help with down payments on our children's first homes. Our parents were generous enough to help with these expenses for us, and we feel it's our responsibility to pay these forward to our kids. If you think about the uses for our insurance proceeds, you should note that nothing on the list is for us, personally. Insurance is not for you. Why? Because you'll be dead. Insurance is for those we leave behind. That being said, I cannot tell you how many single childless clients came to me with large amounts of life insurance. I would always ask them why they have life insurance, and not one of them could answer that simple question.

I know why so many singles have life insurance. It goes back to the way insurance agents are trained and the motivation of the majority of advisors we talked about in Chapter 12. One of the first tasks a financial advisor will be asked to do during training is to create a list of family and friends to make contact with once they pass all the licensing exams. When you get the inevitable call from your old high school buddy, great uncle, or whoever, you will be asked to buy something that may or may not be appropriate for your life situation. If you don't need the product they're selling, don't buy it. You will only be wasting your money and reinforcing their bad behavior. On the motivation of the average financial advisor, let me tell you a little secret. Insurance is the single highest paying product a financial advisor can sell. Consequently, there are a lot of miss sold insurance products. ***What you need to buy if you have a family that relies on your financial support is basic term life coverage.***

Term life coverage is like car insurance. If you have car insurance and you don't get into an accident, then there is no benefit. Term life insurance is exactly the same, unless you die, it's money spent for nothing. It's not wasted though. Insurance coverage gives our family peace of mind. Peace of mind is always worth paying for. I know that if I get taken out by a big rig truck on one the many Los Angeles freeways, my family will be financially covered. Besides term life insurance, there are a lot of life insurance products that have what is referred to as a cash value. What happens with these types of policies is that a portion of your premium goes into an investment bucket, and it grows over time and as you make additional payments towards the policy. On the surface it sounds good; having a portion of your insurance expense building into usable block of funds, but the premiums you pay and the internal cost of those investments are very high. As an example, I got two dummy quotes for a 30 year old male non-smoker with a $500,000 death benefit. 30-year term life had an annual premium of $845 vs. a cash value policy which had an annual premium of $2,390. In most cases, you'd be better off investing the difference in the premiums on your own in a lower cost option. My recommendation is to buy a term policy that covers you only during your working years, and buy it when you are younger. Term policies issued before age 40 are very cheap.

Health insurance is another one of those items that you should pay for and hope you never need. *I beg you to always carry health insurance for yourself and your family.* Even though it has recently become the law of the land to have medical insurance, many still choose not to buy it. When my older son was 18 years old, he was in an car wreck that totaled his vehicle and resulted in a compound fracture of his right leg. For those of you who don't know what a compound fracture is; it's when a broken bone breaks through the skin. Let me tell you that seeing 4 inches of your son's tibia sticking out of his shin is not a pretty picture. After two weeks in the hospital, four reconstructive surgeries and over a year of physical therapy, the medical bills were staggering. I stopped adding the bills once they breeched $120,000. If we had to pay all those bills, it would have set us back by a decade on our savings. Since we had medical coverage, the entire expense was covered with only a couple hundred dollars out of pocket.

On the other hand, I had a client whose adult daughter **CHOSE** not to buy medical insurance even though she could have. Unfortunately, the daughter developed cancer which required chemo therapy and radiation treatments. Just like my son, the bills were staggering. Unfortunately, since there was no insurance, my client was forced to liquidate all of her investments to help her daughter. My retired client is now completely broke. Here is the moral of this story. *If you choose not to carry health insurance, then you are not only risking your own financial future, but also your entire family's.* While they do exist, there are not too many parents that would opt to let their child die for lack of money, so don't put them into the situation where they wipe themselves out because of you.

I have to confess that I do not have a great level of expertise when it comes to the details of health insurance. My wife and I have always purchased it through our employers. Our family has been very satisfied with the Health Maintenance Organization (HMO) option. The participant in this type of plan has to use a limited (in network) number of doctors, and if you need to see a specialist, your primary care physician needs to approve the visit prior to you going in order for your insurance to cover the expense. The HMO is typically the lowest cost option offered through an employer or purchased individually. There are also Preferred Provider Organizations (PPO) and Traditional Indemnity plans that allow access to a far wider stable of primary care physicians and specialists. Your insurance cost and out of pocket expense (co-payments) will be higher for these types of plans. If you or a family member has a condition that requires a higher level of care, then these plans may be for you.

What if you are young, healthy and work for an employer who doesn't offer health benefits? I remember when I was young and bullet-proof. Why should we pay for medical insurance when we never go see the doctor? Mathematically, you're right. Odds are that this will be money spent, but not used. In addition, paying the fines for not having insurance is usually cheaper than the insurance. Remember two things; my son's accident and paying for peace of mind is always worth the cost. If this is your situation, look into what is called catastrophic health insurance coverage. The way these plans work is that roughly the first $5000 of cost in any year is covered by you out of pocket. Once your bills exceed this amount, then the insurance covers everything else. For my son's accident, if we were covered with this type of plan, we would have written a check for $5,000 and the insurance company would have covered the other $115,000+. The advantage of the catastrophic coverage is that the premiums you pay are relatively low.

Take responsibility and get yourself some form of medical coverage. If you have a family or others that rely on your support, get yourself some term life insurance as well. I hope you don't need either one, but in case you do, health and life insurance will protect those whom you care about most.

Chapter 15

Buying Property: The Basics and Alternatives to the 30-year Fixed Rate

As was discussed in Chapter 4, buying real estate can really solidify your financial situation. Let's spend a little extra time on this topic, so you'll understand in a little more detail the process of buying residential real estate. The writing of this guidebook closely follows one of the worst housing market crises in recent times. It was caused by a number of factors including extremely lax rules for lending and creating mortgage bonds as well as wide spread speculation (gambling) on housing prices. The aftermath of the crisis created an environment of extremely tight lender and government rules for real estate which will likely ease with the passage of time. Despite the crisis and tighter standards, the fundamental value of buying real estate has not changed. For our purposes, and because of state and regional differences, we'll try to stick to generalities rather than overly specifics guidelines. The first step in the home buying process is to get a prequalification letter.

Prequalification is really important because it will let you know definitively what you can afford to purchase and

narrow your home search accordingly. The process entails you sitting down with a mortgage banker or broker and give them proof of income, cash reserves, down payment source and amount, detailing your current debt (Chapters 3 and 4) and letting them run your credit score (Chapter 5). Based on these factors, they will generate a letter stating how much of a purchase price and a total loan amount for which you could qualify. While the prequalification is not a guarantee that the lender will fund a loan, it is a very strong credential to present to a real estate agent and more importantly, the seller of a property. The critical components of determining your manageable purchase price are your income, the size of your down payment and the type of mortgage you choose. Since the income we earn is somewhat out of our control, let's take a look at the second two factors now.

The majority of us are going to have to come up with a down payment in order to make an offer to purchase property. The exception is for military veterans who opt for a Veterans Administration (VA) loan. Other than that exception, lenders and sellers will require a down payment. The magic threshold for a down payment is 20% of the purchase price. If you're thinking about homes priced in the $250,000 range, it is preferable to make the purchase with a down payment of $50,000. Why is 20% an ideal number? Currently, anything less will subject the purchaser to Private Mortgage Insurance (PMI). PMI is a borrower paid insurance policy that protects the lender in case of mortgage default (failure to pay). PMI can be fairly expensive. Cost can exceed 1% of the loan amount pre year. Therefore, on that $250,000 purchase with only a $10,000 down payment, PMI could cost approximately $2400/year which would add an extra $200 to the monthly payment. PMI is supposed to end once you have 20% equity in the property, but can remain until you have as much as 50% equity. If you decide to accept a deal that requires PMI, read the fine print and know when you will be able stop paying the extra insurance cost.

Be aware that not having the full 20% down payment will also result in you paying a higher interest rate for your loan. Currently, interest rates are about a half of a percent higher for a loan with only a 10% down payment compared to the standard 20%. Using 10% down on a purchase price of $250,000, the 30-year fixed rate loan rate will move from 4% to 4.50% and will result in a payment that is $66 higher per month (plus $188 for PMI). $254 is a substantial increase, so *if it is at all possible to get your down payment up to the 20% threshold, do it.* The other critical factor to determining affordability for the prequalification letter is the type of loan. There are many different loans offered by financial institutions in addition to the standard 30-year fixed type. As a perspective property buyer, you get to choose the type of loan used to prequalify you for the purchase.

The only example used in Chapter 4 was the 30 year fixed, but there are many alternatives. In the fixed rate realm, you may opt to pay off your house over 20, 15 or 10 years. There are also customizable loans where one could opt, for example, for a 17 year loan. The downside of shortening the term of the loan is that it will result in a higher monthly payment. A higher monthly payment will lower the loan amount for which you would qualify given the same amount of income. The upsides of choosing a shorter term are twofold. First, the interest rate you pay is going to be less. Recall the same principle holds true with bonds. The shorter the term (of a loan or a bond) equates to less risk to the lender, and therefore the interest rate will be lower. The other benefit of choosing a shorter term is that the total interest you will pay over the course of the loan is going to be substantially less. Take a look at the table on the following page. At the time of writing, mortgage rates are at historic lows, but the principles described above are still well illustrated. Rates used were the mean of those published as of the writing of this chapter.[xiii] The rates below assume a $250,000 purchase price, $50,000 (20%) down payment, $200,000 loan amount and a credit score greater than 739.

Years	Rate	Payment	Total Payments	Total Interest
10	2.675%	$ 1,901.36	$ 228,162.70	$ 28,162.70
15	2.875%	$ 1,369.17	$ 246,450.86	$ 46,450.86
20	3.250%	$ 1,134.39	$ 272,253.97	$ 72,253.97
30	3.500%	$ 898.09	$ 323,312.18	$ 123,312.18

Note how the rate increases as the term of the loan gets longer, but the monthly payment goes down. Also, see that the shorter duration loans have substantially lower total interest cost. ***If you have the income to comfortably manage a higher monthly payment, the interest savings will be substantial.***

The other types of mortgage aside from the fixed rate type are variable rate. As the name implies, the rates can (and probably will) change over time. I am not a fan of these types of mortgages, and would only recommend using them if one **knew** that they would only be in the property for a short period of time. If you are on a temporary job assignment or were buying a property to improve it and re-sell for a quick profit, then you may want to consider a variable rate mortgage. The reason I do not recommend the variable rate is their lack of certainty. Nobody has a crystal ball in terms of knowing when and by how much interest rates will change. In finance and in life, you should avoid making any commitment that you potentially are not able to keep.

Variable rate mortgages were another factor contributing to the real estate debacle that closely followed the stock market crash. What happened to a lot of folks was they got into houses with little money down and agreed to mortgages they could only afford at the low variable rate. Their plan was to refinance once the interest rate on their loan started to float.

Unfortunately, home prices went down, and lenders would not give loans to borrowers who owed more than their home was worth. As the variable rates re-set to higher levels, people could no longer afford to make the higher payments. They walked away from their properties by the thousands.

As was alluded to above, the benefit to the variable mortgage is that the initial rates and payments for this type of loan are lower than the 30-year fixed. They allow a buyer to qualify for more house than they otherwise could. Keep in mind that this can be both good and bad as we just went through. To illustrate the benefit of the variable let's take a look at the common 5/1 Adjustable Rate Mortgage (ARM). The structure of the loan is that the payment will be fixed for the first 5 years, and then adjust for the remaining 25 years. Rates for this type of loan are currently a full percent lower than the 30-year fixed option. Using the same parameters that were used for the table above, the monthly payment would be about $100 less per month than the 30 year fixed. Because of this lower payment, the buyer opting for a variable rate could qualify for a larger loan amount with the same amount of income and percentage down payment. The options for variable rates are 3/1, 5/1, 7/1 and 10/1. These have fixed rates for 3, 5, 7 and 10 years, respectively, then the rate floats for the remainder of the loan term. How exactly the rates float after the fixed period varies widely by lender. Most are tied to one of a number of published interest rate indexes.

There are also "interest-only" varieties of the 3, 5, 7 year variable rate mortgages. Interest only loans will have the absolute lowest payment of all the variable rate loans because the borrower is not paying anything towards the amount borrowed. On a 5/1 interest only at 4%, the same borrower detailed above would have a payment of only $667. This lower payment would balloon the loan amount for which they could qualify. The significant drawback of this option is that after making 5 years of payments totaling $40,000 the borrower would still owe the lender the same $200,000. *Take advantage of the lower payments offered by variable rate mortgages only if you are in a situation where you will be holding onto the house for less than the fixed portion of the loan*. If you are going to buy a family home where you will be staying for the foreseeable future, don't take the risk that a variable rate mortgage inherently has.

After a fairly long mortgage detour, we are back to the buying process. We know how much of a down payment we will make and have picked the type of mortgage that is most appropriate for our situation. We must now find the property on which we want to make an offer. You may want to enlist the services of a real estate agent at this point. He or she can take you to a number of different possibilities that meet your needs and budget. When choosing a property to buy, *the most important element to the current and future value is location*. A spectacular home in a crappy neighborhood will likely be less valuable than a beat-up home in a great neighborhood. The general rule for buying property is to seek out the worst home on the best block. As you bring that worst house up to the standards of the neighborhood, your equity should go up tremendously. Regardless of whether you have, are planning to have or do not want to have children, be aware of the reputation of the schools in the neighborhood you're considering. Neighborhoods that feed into schools with the best reputation will be more expensive, but will retain and go up in value faster than a comparable house without a quality school system.

In addition to location, another choice a homebuyer will face is whether to buy a single family home (stand-alone structure without any shared walls) or a townhouse/condominium (shared walls with another property owner). As has been detailed throughout this book, this type of choice comes with both positives and negatives. For the most part, a single family residence will rise in value faster when housing prices are going up and will hold its value better when real estate prices are falling. The condominium offers the advantages of a lower purchase price and reduced time and effort on maintenance. Typically, landscaping and exterior structural maintenance are done by the homeowner's association. This benefit comes at the expense of higher monthly homeowner's dues.

Association dues for a community of single family homes will usually be lower because all the landscaping and maintenance for the home is the responsibility of the individual homeowner. One part of your investigation of any property that has a homeowner's association is to walk the common areas (clubhouse, pools, parks, etc.) to see whether they are in good repair. Most associations have the right to bill all homeowners in the community a special assessment to cover extraordinary costs. If you are a homeowner in the community, you will have no choice but to pay your portion of a potentially large repair bill. Another item to look at is whether the association has amassed sufficient reserve funds. Reserve funds are a block of liquid cash controlled by the homeowners association which are used to maintain and/or replace all the common property and facilities. If you find that reserve funds are less than 80% of what is required, then this should be an area of concern. Less than 60% should be a deal breaker. You can see the status of the association reserves by a review of their most recent financial statements which will be available at your request.

One last note on associations; all have a set of rules called Covenants, Conditions and Restrictions (CC&R's). These rules limit the scope of how you can use the property and how you must maintain the exterior appearance of the property. If you are planning to paint your house bright pink, keep multiple animals, run a business out of your home, etc., then make sure the CC&Rs permit such uses. Once you have done all your homework on a particular piece of property and you find it meets you needs and is affordable, then you will make a written offer to purchase the property.

A real estate agent will have a standardized form on which you will put in the terms and the price you are willing to pay for the property. Keep in mind that this is a negotiation between you and the seller. You have the right to offer whatever price you deem fair regardless of the published asking price. Any item that you want to remain with the property (like a built in refrigerator or washer/dryer) should be specified in your offer. Expenses like escrow and title can be the responsibility of either buyer or seller and will be specified in your offer to purchase. After you make your offer, the current owner will have the option to accept your offer as is, counter your proposal with one of their own or flat out reject your offer. This process can go back and forth several times before the buyer and seller either reach an agreement or decide to give up on the deal. Once you have an agreed upon offer, you are going to enter escrow to close the purchase.

Escrow is a multi-step process to complete the purchase of the property. During escrow, you will officially apply for the loan for which you were prequalified. The lender will invariably require additional documentation beyond what you provided during prequalification. The lender will also order an appraisal of the property. It is critical that the appraised value is equal to or greater than the agreed upon purchase price. If the appraisal comes in lower than the purchase price, then the lender may want you to come into the deal with a larger down payment than you had initially planned. During escrow, the seller will have to disclose any material items affecting the value and usability of the property. The buyer will acknowledge and accept these disclosures. Separately, the buyer may (should) request any number of home inspections to insure that there are no hidden defects within the property. These inspections could include a basic home inspection of the structure and fixtures, a pest inspection, environmental inspection, earthquake/and or flood reports, etc. Your agent should help with the list of inspections that are appropriate to the region in which you plan to buy. During escrow, you will buy homeowners insurance. Property insurance is required by every lender. Another lender requirement that is to your benefit as well is title insurance. This will insure that the seller actually owns the property and that nobody else has an ownership interest or claim to the property.

Just before closing on your purchase, it is a good idea to do a final walk-through of the property to make sure that all agreed upon items to remain in the house are still present and that there is no new damage to the property. Finally, when all these items are completed, you will receive a mandatory form called a HUD-1. This form will detail the purchase price, down payment, financing costs as well as every other cost and fee associated with the purchase. Review the form for accuracy. Assuming all is ok with the HUD-1, you will close the deal by sitting down with a notary (or an attorney in some states) to sign a literal mountain of paperwork. After a couple of days where money moves from your and the lender's accounts to the seller and the deed to the property is recorded, the deal closes. Congratulations, you are now the property owner.

As a final note on the topic of home buying, let's spend a moment on using a real estate agent. My opinion of realtors mirrors that of financial advisors (Chapter 12). Of course, if you are relocating to a new city, the local knowledge a real estate agent should possess will be invaluable in regards to picking an appropriate neighborhood and home that meets your needs. Just know that they may not necessarily recommend the best choice nor negotiate the best possible deal on your behalf. In California, unless you are paying a real estate agent a separate finder's or agent fee, your agent's first responsibility is to the seller of the property even if they are representing you in the transaction. In addition, never forget that agents are only paid when a deal closes. Because of this, the agent may cut corners and/or not negotiate too aggressively in order to get a deal done. I am not saying that all realtors will try to take advantage of their position. Rather,

I want you to know how they are paid so you will be aware of the conflict of interest they have while they're negotiating on your behalf. The same advice I gave you in Chapters 10 and 12 about trusting your gut and picking a financial advisor apply to your selection of a real estate agent.

*****

Thank you for investing some of your valuable time into reading this guidebook. Now you know more about financial matters than 90% of the public. No kidding, that's the straight up truth. It is not overly complex, but it is just never taught to us in a concise manner. That is exactly why I set out to lay down these basics for you. I hope you understand that the lessons here will make you rich. It's not a scheme that will happen overnight. It's more about creating a discipline that will serve you a lifetime. I wish you the very best luck, happiness in your pursuits and the financial freedom to live your life the way you choose.

END NOTES

---

[i] For those of you who whipped out your calculators and multiplied out our example actually came up with the a number slightly less than the a full double ($175.67), This discrepancy is due to annual compounding rather than daily or more frequent compounding which is how most banks and insurance companies credit their interest.

[ii] 50/50 index stock/bond portfolio earned an average of 9% over the 60 year period 1950 to 2010. Subtract 2% for investment costs

[iii] U.S. Department of Education, National Center for Education Statistics. (2011). *The Condition of Education, 2011*

[iv] JPMorgan Guide to the Markets, 6/30/2012, page 60

[v] Ibid

[vi] Ibid

[vii] Assume we make our account half stock and half bonds. From 1950 to 2011, the actual return on this 50/50 account was 8.9%[vii]. With the 50/50 strategy, we would have earned about 82% of the total return of the all stock account (8.9% on the 50/50 account divided by 10.9% return on the all stock account). The range of possibilities (or risk) over that 62 years for the 50/50 strategy account was +32% in the best year and -15% in the worst.[vii] The total range of outcomes is 47 (32% to the positive + 15% to the negative = 47). Compare that to the all-stock portfolio having a range of possibilities of 88 (51% to the positive + 37% to the negative = 88). Comparing the two ranges representing risk, we find that we expose our half stock half bond account to only 53% of the risk of an all stock account (47 divided by 88).

[viii] Rate was estimated using the average rate on the constant maturity 3-month treasury bill data from 1992 to 2011 published by the Federal Reserve.

[ix] Rate was an average rate of CPI data from 1992 to 2011 published by the Bureau of Labor Statistics.

[x] "Determinants of Portfolio Performance" Gary Brinson, Randolph Hood, G Beebower. *Financial Analysts Journal, May-June1986. Association for Investment Management Research.*

[xi] Charts show 11/19/2008 to 09/07/2012 dividend adjusted daily closing price data taken from Yahoo Finance for the following securities AOK for low risk, AOM for moderate risk, AOA for aggressive risk and IOO for all stock. Note that IOO prices were divided by 2 to keep chart scales consistent. Asset allocations percentages based on Q2 fact sheets published on iShares website.

[xii] Vanguard's website is www.vanguard.com and Fidelity's website is www.fidelity.com

[xiii] Rates used were from the Los Angeles area. Rates shown in the table were the median rate of those published by Yahoo Finance found at finance.yahoo.com/rates on October 4, 2012

www.ingramcontent.com/pod-product-compliance
Lightning Source LLC
Chambersburg PA
CBHW022108170526
45157CB00004B/1535